D0461493

democracy

**mc** **Marshall Cavendish**
Benchmark
New York

# democracy

## TOM LANSFORD

Marshall Cavendish Benchmark
99 White Plains Road • Tarrytown, NY
10591 • www.marshallcavendish.us
Copyright © 2008 by Marshall Cavendish
Corporation • Maps Copyright © 2008
by Marshall Cavendish Corporation
Maps by XNR Productions, Inc.
• Lansford, Tom.

Democracy / Tom Lansford. • p. cm.
— (Political systems of the world) •
Summary: "Gives an overview of
democracy as a political system,
including an historical discussion of
democracies throughout the world"-
Provided by publisher. • Includes
bibliographical references and index.
ISBN-13: 978-0-7614-2629-5 • 1.
Democracy-Juvenile literature. I. Title.
II. Series. • JC423.L344 2007 • 321.8-
dc22 2006025351 • Photo research by
Connie Gardner

Cover photo by Joe Sohm/The Image Works
Photographs in this book are used by
permission and through the courtesy of:
*Image Works:* Joe Sohm, back cover, 1,
2–3, 8; Jim West, 105; Robin Weiner/Wire
Pix, 106; *The Granger Collection*: 11, 34,
36, 55; *Corbis*: Dan Habib, 13; Bettmann,
20, 27, 61, 92; Tim Graham, 49; Pedro
Armestre/epa, 67; Lee Besford/Reuters,
70; Christopher Morris, 75; Toman Lou,
83; *Magnum Photos:* Ian Berry, 24; Renee
Burri, 87; *Getty*: Image News, 99.
Publisher: Michelle Bisson
Art Director: Anahid Hamparian
Series Designer: Sonia Chaghatzbanian
Printed in Malaysia
1 3 5 6 4 2

# Contents

democracy

# The Elements of Democracy

**1**

THE MOST COMMON FORM OF GOVERNMENT in the world today is a democracy. Democracy is a system in which the people control political power. The word democracy comes from two Greek words, *demos*, or "people," and *cracy*, or "rule of." Democracy can thus be translated literally as "rule of the people." In the United States, many assume democracy means "government of the people, by the people, and for the people," as Abraham Lincoln stated in his Gettysburg Address. This concept means that the ultimate authority over governmental policies and decisions rests with the people.

Democracy emerged as a political system in response to increasing demand from ordinary citizens for a voice in the government. Its principal purpose is to overcome tyranny, or rule by a single individual or small group. By giving ultimate political authority to the people, democracy disperses power and prevents the rise of dictatorship or other forms of authoritarian government. In addition, democracy is perceived as the best way to ensure equality and liberty for all people in a society. Democracy allows people to voice their frustrations or problems through a regulated process so that the government can seek solutions to address these issues.

# The Gettysburg Address

On November 19, 1863, Abraham Lincoln delivered this address at the dedication of the Soldiers' National Cemetery at Gettysburg, just over four months after the Battle of Gettysburg, to affirm the importance of democracy and liberty for all in the United States:

> Four score and seven years ago our fathers brought forth on this continent a new nation, conceived in Liberty, and dedicated to the proposition that all men are created equal.
>
> Now we are engaged in a great civil war, testing whether that nation or any nation, so conceived and so dedicated, can long endure. We are met on a great battlefield of that war. We have come to dedicate a portion of that field as a final resting-place for those who here gave their lives that this nation might live. It is altogether fitting and proper that we should do this.
>
> But, in a larger sense, we cannot dedicate . . . we cannot consecrate . . . we cannot hallow . . . this ground. The brave men, living and dead, who struggled here, have consecrated it far above our poor power to add or detract. The world will little note nor long remember what we say here, but it can never forget what they did here. It is for us, the living, rather, to be dedicated here to the unfinished work which they who fought here have thus far so nobly advanced. It is rather for us to be here dedicated to the great task remaining before us . . . that

This 1905 lithograph depicts President Abraham Lincoln delivering the Gettysburg Address on November 19, 1863.

from these honored dead we take increased devotion to that cause for which they gave the last full measure of devotion; . . . that we here highly resolve that these dead shall not have died in vain; that this nation, under God, shall have a new birth of freedom; and that government of the people, by the people, for the people, shall not perish from the earth.

Modern democracies have a number of characteristics. All allow citizens more or less equal access to political power through elections and equitable voting rights. All also promote equality by not favoring one group over another. Democracies further allow citizens to control the political process. The main concerns and issues of the majority of the people must be addressed by the government. Democracies must also have active citizen participation and regular elections.

Nonetheless, there are many different types of democracies. There are also various ways to arrange democratic governments. Societies may put limitations on political participation in democracies or arrange for systems in which people transfer their power through elections to others to make decisions for them. In addition, democracy can exist on a variety of levels, including local and national levels.

## FORMS OF DEMOCRACY

There are two basic forms of democracy: direct and representative. A direct democracy is one in which all of the citizens of a political organization jointly make all decisions for that body. When an issue must be decided, all citizens gather in an assembly and vote for or against the item. One example of a direct democracy is ancient Athens. Any time the government needed to make a choice, all of the citizens came together, debated the issue, and then voted. The main advantages to direct democracy are that all citizens feel included in the political process and that all decisions have a high degree of legitimacy.

### Direct Democracy

Direct democracy has a number of disadvantages that limit its appeal. First, it is impractical for large countries. It would be impossible for a country such as India, with a population of more than one billion, to have everyone meet or provide a forum to discuss issues. This is also true for medium-sized countries such as France or the United Kingdom, which each have populations of about sixty million. Second, direct democracies require high levels of citizen participation, and most people in today's world do not have the time to study all of the issues so that they can cast informed votes. Third, in the past, direct democracies often actually constrained popular participation by limiting who could be a citizen. For example, in Athens, women

All is not always serious at town meetings. In the New England town of Webster, New Hampshire, citizens share a laugh during the presentation of gag gifts for a local representative.

and slaves were not given the status of citizens. Fourth, and finally, direct democracies can lead to the tyranny of the majority. On the one hand, majority rule is important for the successful functioning of a government, but sometimes majorities can trample on minority rights. The tyranny of the majority refers to a situation in which a majority population unfairly represses minority groups. The majority could be an ethnic, a religious, or even an economic group. For much of American history, the rights of ethnic minorities such as African Americans were suppressed by the majority white population.

Today, direct democracy is mainly found at the local and regional levels. Many towns and villages around the world still allow all citizens to debate and vote on issues. In the United States, the town hall meeting, common in New England, is one form of direct democracy. There are other manifestations of direct democracy, but these are usually issue-specific. Many governments use referendums, in which citizens vote directly on a particular issue, as a means of deciding important or controversial items. For instance, in 2005, in France, voters decided in a national referendum to reject a proposed constitution for the European Union, of which France is a member. In some cases, citizens may even initiate a referendum if they are able to collect the required number of signatures. As an example, in California, since 1911, citizens have been able to place an issue on ballots if they are able to collect signatures equal to 5 percent of the voters in the previous election for changes to state law or 8 percent for changes to the state constitution. One other form of direct democracy is the recall, which allows voters to force a politician out of office. The recall is rarely used, but in 2003, voters in California recalled Governor Gray Davis and replaced him with actor-turned-politician Arnold Schwarzenegger.

## Representative Democracy

The second form of democracy is representative democracy. In this form of democracy, people choose officials to represent their interests and to make decisions on their behalf. This is usually accomplished through regular elections in which candidates seek executive or legislative office. The people still hold ultimate authority over the government, but elected officials develop, implement, and enforce laws and policies. National governments that are based on the principle

# John Quincy Adams, Inaugural Address
## (Friday, March 4, 1825)

In his inaugural speech, President John Quincy Adams spoke about the value of representative democracy for promoting national unity, easing regional differences, and encouraging cooperation on major issues:

> The prejudices everywhere too commonly entertained against distant strangers are worn away, and the jealousies of jarring interests are allayed by the composition and functions of the great national councils annually assembled from all quarters of the Union at this place. Here the distinguished men from every section of our country, while meeting to deliberate upon the great interests of those by whom they are deputed, learn to estimate the talents and do justice to the virtues of each other. The harmony of the nation is promoted and the whole Union is knit together by the sentiments of mutual respect, the habits of social intercourse, and the ties of personal friendship formed between the representatives of its several parts in the performance of their service at this metropolis.

of representative democracy are usually referred to as republics. The majority of most democratic governments in the world today are republics, including the United States, Mexico, and most European countries. An official can be elected as the leader of a government, often known as a president or premier, or to a legislature that creates laws and policy. Examples of legislatures include the United States Congress, the British Parliament, or the French National Assembly. In addition, all states in this country have a legislature. Some areas even have elected judges.

Representative democracy has several advantages over direct democracy. First, elected officials can concentrate on politics and, therefore, become specialists on issues in a way that most average people cannot because they do not have the time or resources. Second, by limiting the number of people who debate and decide matters, the process to enact legislation is quicker than direct democracy. Third, by only having elections every few years, countries save time and money on campaigning, whereas in direct democracies there would be campaigns for and against most issues. Fourth, elected officials often provide continuity in government and prevent radical changes in policy. Fifth, and finally, representatives can make difficult choices that the public might avoid. For example, voters are usually very reluctant to endorse tax increases, even if they are necessary. Many argue that in a direct democracy, voters would seldom approve tax increases. Representative democracy also is less likely to result in the tyranny of the majority, although this depends on the types of delegates elected to represent the people.

Most elected representatives can be divided into three philosophical categories or styles. The delegate votes and acts in accordance with the wishes of his or her constituency. This type of representative is faithful to the voters and does not embrace positions with which the majority of voters disagree. Delegates believe their role is to always vote in line with the preferences of their constituency, even if they privately disagree with the specific policy. Trustees follow policies that seem the best, even if they are not popular with the public. Trustees often take principled stances on issues even if it costs votes or support. Trustees often use their own initiative and emerge as leaders within legislatures. They also are often turned out of office faster than their counterparts. The politico combines the main traits of both the delegate and the trustee. This type of representative will sometimes follow the wishes of his or her constituency, but will also oppose the majority if he or she believes the issue to be important.

Representative democracy also has drawbacks. Like direct democracy, it requires the participation of its citizens, although to a lesser degree. One problem faced by many contemporary representative democracies is growing voter apathy in which citizens feel disenfranchised and are consequently less likely to vote. In the United States, in many elections less than half of those eligible to vote actually do so. If people do not feel that their vote counts, they are less likely to pay attention to the actions of their representatives. This causes problems for the representatives as they try to understand where their constituents stand on specific issues (this is especially problematic for representatives who follow the delegate model described above). Another major problem for representative democracy is the potential for officials to become disengaged from their constituents and unduly influenced by lobbyists or special interest groups. Many political thinkers have argued that the more remote people become from interaction with government, the greater the danger that corruption and governmental inaction will become prevalent.

## LIMITED AND FULL DEMOCRACIES

Democracies give political power to the citizens of a country, but rules and restrictions about citizenship can exclude some people and groups from participating in the democratic process. Governments that prevent segments of the population from engaging in politics are known as limited democracies. Limited democracies often discriminate against certain groups because of ethnic, religious, gender, or economic circumstances. For instance, through most of its history, the United States was a limited democracy. Women were not allowed to vote until 1920, and many minorities were prevented from voting by state and local officials until the 1960s. This was in spite of the fact that the United States made it relatively easy for people to become citizens either by being born on American territory or by spending a specific amount of time in the country.

# The Abolition of the Poll Tax: The Twenty-fourth Amendment

One way in which state, county, and city governments in the United States attempted to prevent groups from voting was through the poll tax, a fee that had to be paid in order to vote. For poor people, the poll tax was a major obstacle to voting for many years until the civil rights movement of the 1960s. The poll tax was repealed in the United States in 1964 through the Twenty-fourth Amendment:

Twenty-fourth Amendment

Section 1. The right of citizens of the United States to vote in any primary or other election for President or Vice President, for electors for President or Vice President, or for Senator or Representative in Congress, shall not be denied or abridged by the United States or any State by reason of failure to pay any poll tax or other tax.

Section 2. The Congress shall have power to enforce this article by appropriate legislation.

In contrast, other countries make it very difficult for immigrants to become citizens. For instance, in France, children born in the country to immigrant parents must apply for citizenship when they become an adult (they are not considered French citizens until their application is approved). The same is true in Germany, although immigrant children are eligible for citizenship if one of their parents has been a legal resident for a specified period of time and the child applies for citizenship before the age of twenty-three.

Sometimes governments pass laws that limit the ability of people to vote without expressly stating that this is the purpose of the law, in order to discriminate against groups of people. For instance, in the United States after the Civil War, many states passed laws that were designed to prevent African Americans from voting. Since the Fifteenth Amendment to the Constitution forbade discrimination based on race, state governments used other kinds of laws to deprive minority groups of their ability to vote. One measure was known as the poll tax. It required individuals to pay a fee in order to vote. Another measure was the literacy test, which required citizens to be able to read and write before they could register to vote. Since slaves were forbidden by law from learning to read and write, the literacy test meant that most of the newly freed slaves could not vote. Later, as education became more available, white officials commonly flunked minority applicants even if they scored high enough on the literacy test to pass. In one famous incident, an African American who had a doctorate degree from Harvard University was denied his request to register to vote because a white official claimed he had failed a literacy test (although a copy of the test clearly showed he actually had a perfect score).

Some countries are democratic at the local, or regional level, but not at all levels of government. In China, local elections are held for mayor and town councils, but there are no national elections. In other countries, democracy is limited by structures within the government. Iran could be considered a representative democracy since officials are elected to a national legislature; however, the laws passed by that body have to be approved by a council of religious leaders. Democracy can be limited by groups within a society. In some countries, government-sponsored groups attempt

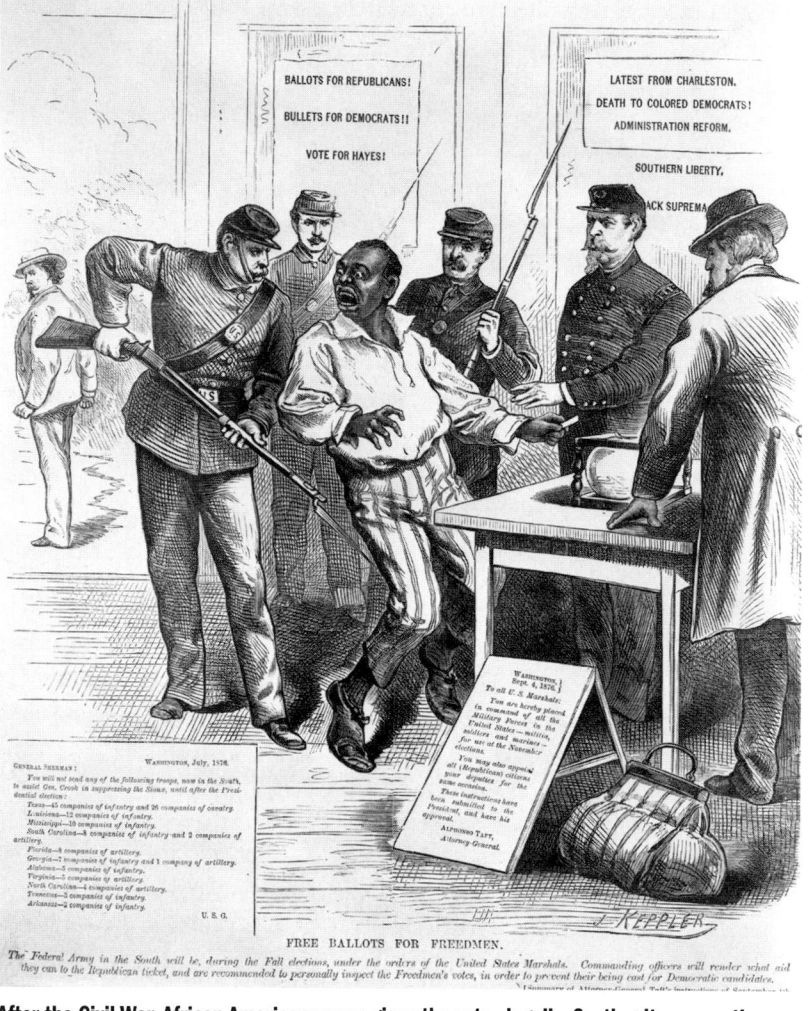

FREE BALLOTS FOR FREEDMEN.

The Federal Army in the South will be, during the Fall elections, under the orders of the United States Marshals. Commanding officers will render what aid they can to the Republican ticket, and are recommended to personally inspect the Freedmen's votes, in order to prevent their being cast for Democratic candidates.

**After the Civil War, African Americans were given the vote—legally. Casting it was another matter. This illustration shows a black citizen accosted by soldiers as he tries to vote.**

to frighten or intimidate voters to make sure that their candidates win elections.

Limited democracies may constrain the political power of people in unofficial ways. For instance, sometimes one political party dominates a system and rivals are unable to be elected. In Japan, Mexico, and Taiwan, for most of the 1900s, each country's political leaders came from a single party within those nations (the Liberal Democratic Party in Japan, the Institutional Revolutionary Party, or PRI, in Mexico, and the Nationalist Party in Taiwan). Without competition between political parties, people are unable to promote new ideas and approaches to problem-solving. Even if free elections are held at all levels of government and voting rights are widespread, if there is only one dominant or official political party, a country is considered a limited democracy.

Full democracies are based on the twin principles of political equality and equal opportunity. Political equality means that all citizens have the right to vote and that all can participate in political activities without discrimination. Full democracies allow all or almost all of their citizens to vote. These systems have universal suffrage, which means that all citizens have the right to vote. In addition, everyone's vote must count equally when tabulations are being made after an election for a specific office. Only under extraordinary circumstances should a person have his or her right to vote taken away. The government must have a compelling reason to take away a person's voting privilege and cannot exclude a group, only specific individuals. Among the reasons that some governments remove voting rights for individuals include conviction of serious crimes.

Full democracies must also provide equal opportunity for all citizens. This means that all groups should have the same political, economic, and social rights as other groups. For example, everyone should have the same influence in politics. Officials should not favor one group over another when it comes to resources or societal rewards. All groups should have the same opportunities. Everyone in a society must be able to progress economically and socially according to his or her own abilities and desires. All people must have equal education as well. Governments that fail to provide every group with the same opportunities are not considered full democracies. Differences between limited and full democracies will continue to be discussed in the following chapters since such disparities have plagued efforts to develop democracies throughout history.

# History

THROUGHOUT HISTORY, PEOPLE HAVE STRUGGLED against different forms of repression in an effort to gain a voice in the political process. Democracy, especially direct democracy, has been around for most of human history, but it has only recently become a common way to organize large governments and gained acceptance as the fairest way to organize political systems. Instead, democracy has often been seen as dangerous and inefficient. This was because the leaders or elites (the people who have the majority of political or economic power) in societies distrusted their fellow citizens and believed them unworthy of participation in the governing process. The result was that few governments were organized on democratic principles, and those that were, were limited democracies.

## THE ATHENIAN MODEL

The earliest recorded democracies were the ancient Greek city-states. Chios was the first city-state to develop into a democracy, but Athens is the best-known democracy of the period. By 550 BCE, Athens, a city-state of some forty-five thousand people, had a functioning direct democracy. All policies and decisions, including those created by the city's ruling council, were put before the citizens of Athens to approve or reject. Because most men were reluctant to be away from jobs or

Greece was the home of the first known democracies. The Acropolis was built to represent an ideal of civilization.

businesses to serve on the unpaid council, the ruling council was chosen by a lottery. The council was composed of five hundred citizens, and members served for a year. The council proposed legislation and policies that were then put before the citizens to debate and decide through voting. The Athenian model of direct democracy would be adopted by many other Greek city-states. Such a localized democracy also occurred elsewhere in many areas of the world, including India. As Alexander the Great (356–323 BCE) campaigned in India, his army encountered numerous towns and cities with democratic systems similar to that of the Greeks.

Citizenship, and therefore voting rights, was limited in Athens. Slaves, foreigners, new immigrants, and women were excluded from citizenship. Other city-states that had democratic systems placed even greater limitations on citizenship. In some cities, males had to own extensive property to be a citizen, while in other areas they had to at least own their own houses. In most of the city-states, including Athens, only about 20 percent of the male population could vote. Because of the extensive time commitment needed to discuss and vote on issues, many citizens avoided participation, so the true effectiveness of the system was limited. For these reasons, the early Greek systems were limited democracies.

### Plato and Aristotle

Although they were limited democracies, the ancient Greek city-states did provide models for future democracies. In addition, philosophers and scholars of the time wrote about the problems and benefits of democracies and their works influenced later prominent figures who helped develop important themes and components of democratic theory. Plato (427–347 BCE) was among the most significant of the early Greek philosophers. Plato opposed democracy because he believed that the most efficient form of government was one in which an enlightened despot made decisions for the government based on reason and superior education. Plato argued that democracy led to mob rule in which people forced the government to respond to their own selfish interests instead of enacting policies for the general good. He further believed that democracy always led to conflict, as different groups would inevitably try to take control of the government. Finally, Plato distrusted common, or average, people because the Greek philosopher did not feel that these people had the necessary intelligence to make major decisions.

Aristotle (384–322 BCE) was a student of Plato and agreed with many of his teacher's reservations about democracy, including the fear of mob rule. Aristotle differed from his mentor in that he believed that a limited democracy, which he termed a "polity," was the best form of government. Aristotle's polity was a democracy in which elites ruled on behalf of the general population. He rejected full democracy because he believed that the majority would neglect the needs and interests of smaller groups. Aristotle's philosophy was important in creating the idea that government should exist for the common good of all people. During his time and for centuries afterward, many elites believed that government existed only to benefit them. Rulers treated their states and countries as personal property and cared little for the plight of average people. Although Aristotle did not embrace full democracy, his emphasis on the common good would later form one of the main arguments for democracy.

## THE MIDDLE AGES

The rise of the Roman Empire meant the end of the Greek city-states and ushered in a period of authoritarian rule throughout most of Europe. However, many Roman communities did practice limited democracy at the local level and elected town leaders and representatives. Throughout the Middle Ages, democracy continued to survive at the local level, but regional and national government was normally based on the system of monarchy. The power of the monarchs was bolstered by a concept known as the divine right of kings, whichcontended that the power of monarchs came directly from God. However, even in monarchial systems, kings or princes were often elected. For example, in Poland, the king was elected for life by an assembly of nobles known as the Seym (the Seym later evolved into the Polish parliament). German nobles also occasionally elected their kings.

In other countries, nobles were able to limit the powers of kings and other rulers. In England, in 1215, a group of barons took London by force and compelled King John to meet with them at Runnymede and agree to a number of concessions in an agreement known as the Magna Carta (Great Charter). The long-term importance of the Magna Carta

**The Magna Carta, signed by England's King John in 1215, was a giant step on the road to democracy as practiced today.**

was that it helped establish the principle of government by consent in which systems of government operate only with the approval and authorization of the people. Furthermore, monarchs began to turn to assemblies of nobles for advice and support. These assemblies were the forerunners of modern legislative assemblies, but usually did not meet continuously. They were only called into session when the monarch needed their counsel or help. One of the oldest of these assemblies is the English Parliament. In 1295, King Edward I began the practice of calling together not only the nobles, but also prominent middle-class citizens and officials. During the late Middle Ages and Renaissance, limited democracies became increasingly common at the local level. Several city-states in Italy, including Florence, Genoa, and Venice, practiced a narrow version of democracy in which the rich and elites shared power and decision-making authority based on the Athenian model.

## THE ENLIGHTENMENT

Philosophers during the Enlightenment (1600–1800) began to argue in favor of full democracy. A range of historical factors created the conditions that prompted intellectuals and a growing number of political figures to embrace democracy. The rise of commerce created individuals and families that had great wealth during the Renaissance era in Europe (1400–1600). Many of these people did not belong to the traditional aristocratic classes, but they wanted access to political power. The rising merchant class used its wealth to pressure political leaders to issue charters to towns that created limited democracies such as those in Florence, Genoa, and Venice.

The Protestant Reformation (1500–1650) undermined the power and prestige of the Catholic Church and, consequently, eroded the belief in the divine right of kings. Leaders of the Reformation, such as Martin Luther (1483–1546) and John Calvin (1509–1564) contended that there should be a division between the church and the secular government. In addition, the new Protestant sects were often very egalitarian in nature and promoted equality among people. This was very different from the manner in which the Catholic Church of the day supported the rigid social structure. Finally, as Protestants rebelled against Catholic rulers in Europe, many tried to establish limited democracies as a way of rejecting the traditional social system.

# Poland, the Resolution of 1572

On September 17, 1572, Polish nobles met and issued a proclamation stating that in the future they would elect their king:

> We, the Senators of the Crown, spiritual and temporal, and the knighthood of the palatinates of Cracow and Sandomierz, having met in Wiślica on the thirteenth day of December, for the purpose of reviewing and providing for the needs of our Common wealth on the occasion of this interregnum, recognize that on the death of our Sovereign it is fit and proper for us to consider our freedoms and liberties, perceiving the basis for them to be in the free election of our King and Lord.

> Following the example of our ancestors, and regarding ourselves as their worthy descendants, we pledge ourselves by the good and honest word of knighthood, that we do not wish to depart in any detail from our ancestral custom of electing our Sovereign, as described in our statutes and privileges, which apply to all parts of the Realm equally. Collectively, not excluding any parts of the realm, neither those belonging to it of old, nor those belonging to it now and so confirmed, we intend to proceed freely and jointly to elect our Sovereign, and also not to allow any part of the realm, large or small, to separate, but to elect our Sovereign we promise and pledge.

# The English Bill of Rights (1689)

The Bill of Rights of 1689 guaranteed British citizens a range of rights and freedoms, regardless of class or social standing. Many of these freedoms would form the basis of the U.S. Bill of Rights in 1789. Among the important rights and freedoms in the English Bill of Rights were:

That it is the right of the subjects to petition the king, and all commitments and prosecutions for such petitioning are illegal;

That the raising or keeping a standing army within the kingdom in time of peace, unless it be with consent of Parliament, is against law;

That the subjects which are Protestants may have arms for their defence suitable to their conditions and as allowed by law;

That election of members of Parliament ought to be free;

That the freedom of speech and debates or proceedings in Parliament ought not to be impeached or questioned in any court or place out of Parliament;

That excessive bail ought not to be required, nor excessive fines imposed, nor cruel and unusual punishments inflicted;

That jurors ought to be duly impanelled and returned, and jurors which pass upon men in trials for high treason ought to be freeholders;

That all grants and promises of fines and forfeitures of particular persons before conviction are illegal and void;

And that for redress of all grievances, and for the amending, strengthening and preserving of the laws, Parliaments ought to be held frequently.

One major, lasting influence of British democracy was the policy of establishing legislative assemblies in new colonies. As the British gained colonies in North America and the Caribbean, the royal government allowed the settlers to form self-governing bodies so that decisions about the colonies could be made on the spot. This meant that all of the British colonies in North America and the Caribbean were formed on democratic principles, although voting rights were usually limited to free white male property owners over the age of twenty-one.

*British Democracy*

In England in particular, Parliament played an increasingly important role in governing the country. During the English Civil War (1642–1651), the forces of Parliament overthrew King Charles I (1600–1649) and tried to establish a republic. Although their effort failed, as the government became a dictatorship under Oliver Cromwell, the power of Parliament was confirmed by the civil war, and future British kings were limited in their power. This trend was confirmed by the "Glorious Revolution" in which King James II (1633–1701) was forced to abdicate the throne in 1688.

The next monarch had to accept the 1689 Bill of Rights in order to gain the throne. Although the Parliament of the time remained a limited democratic institution, open only to the wealthy and elites of society, its actions laid the basis for future democratic reforms. The English Bill of Rights was an expression of government by consent, and it assured Parliament a permanent role in future governments. This firmly established the principle of constitutional monarchy by which the British political system has since operated. The English Bill of Rights also guaranteed a range of rights and freedoms to all citizens, regardless of class or status. For instance, the document granted everyone the right to trial by jury and provided some assurances of freedom of religion and speech.

*The Philosophy of Democracy*

A number of philosophers during the Enlightenment period extolled the virtues of, and helped define, modern notions of democracy. British philosopher John Locke (1632–1704) had a profound impact on democratic theories by developing the notions of natural rights, private property, and the social contract. Locke believed that all people were born with natural rights, such as liberty and equality, that preceded government, and that political authorities should not be able to take away these natural freedoms. One right that Locke argued in favor of was the right to personal property. He believed that people should be able to acquire property and wealth and that one of the main functions of the government was to protect property. If the government failed in this duty, Locke contended that people had a right to rebel and overthrow the government. Finally, Locke thought that all political systems should be bound by a contract between the people and the institutions of government that defined the rights of the people and the powers of the government. The English Bill of Rights was an example of a social contract. Locke's view of the social contract was that it served to protect people from the excesses of political bodies, and he argued strongly for limited government. Locke's ideas would later greatly influence the American Revolution.

Charles-Louis de Secondat, Baron de La Bréde et de Montesquieu (1689–1755) articulated the concept that government should have a separation of powers so that power would be divided among different branches of the government. Montesquieu believed this was an important safeguard to prevent tyranny. He argued in favor of the British system of constitutional monarchy. Jean-Jacques Rousseau (1712–1778) believed that just governments only existed with the consent of the people and that all citizens should play a role in the political process. Like Locke, Rousseau believed strongly in the social contract, but he asserted that a government could only function well if it was based on the common good (an argument similar to that made by Aristotle). In *The Social Contract* (1762), Rousseau wrote, "Man is born free, and everywhere he is in chains," as a way to explain that man was born with natural rights, which autocratic governments then stripped away. However, without government, man would descend into anarchy and chaos and be in an even worse situation. Whereas Locke argued for limited government, Rousseau thought government should act to promote equality and opportunity. People would surrender some of their natural rights to the government in exchange for the promotion of the common good. The differences between the philosophies of Locke and Rousseau over the scope of government remain to this day.

## THE AMERICAN AND FRENCH REVOLUTIONS

The British colonies in North America were all established with limited democracy as their governmental system. From the creation of the first permanent British colony at Jamestown in 1607 onward, the principles of democracy, limited government, and government by consent became firmly engrained in colonial culture. Several colonies, including Pennsylvania, Connecticut, and Massachusetts, also adopted social contracts in the form of colonial charters that protected individual rights.

When the British attempted to impose a range of new taxes on the colonies in the 1760s, the colonists resisted. Leaders of the colonies met in Philadelphia in 1774 at the First Continental Congress. The

The French revolutionaries based their manifesto, the Declaration of the Rights of Man, on Jean-Jacques Rousseau's notion that government should exist, not for the elite, but to serve the common good.

Second Continental Congress met a year later and undertook a number of steps that led to the American Revolution. The congress created an army, and many delegates began to call for independence, citing Locke's justification for rebellion when government exceeds its authority. The colonies also gave Virginian Thomas Jefferson (1743–1826) the job of drafting a declaration of independence. The resulting document, ratified by Congress on July 4, 1776, contained many of the principles of early philosophers.

*The Declaration of Independence and the Constitution*

The Declaration of Independence used the rhetoric of full democracy. It asserted that all people were equal, and specifically proclaimed the right to "life, liberty, and the pursuit of happiness." (Jefferson did not use Locke's term "property" since slaves at the time were considered property and he did not want to enshrine slavery in the declaration.) The Declaration of Independence also proclaimed the right of people to rebel against unjust government since political institutions derived their legitimacy and authority from the "consent of the people." After adoption of the document, the colonists engaged in a seven-year (1776–1783) struggle to win their independence.

Many of the themes of the Declaration of Independence were incorporated into the U.S. Constitution (1789), which became the social contract between the American people and the government. The Constitution established a limited government in which there was a separation of powers. Political authority at the national level was divided among three branches of government: 1) a legislative branch that formulated and enacted laws and policies; 2) an executive branch that oversaw the implementation of laws and policies; and 3) a judicial branch that made sure that legislation complied with the Constitution by interpreting the law. The Constitution also created a mechanism to add to or revise its features through an amendment process. The first ten amendments to the Constitution were passed collectively in 1789 and became known as the Bill of Rights, since they detailed the main personal liberties and freedoms of U.S. citizens. Many of these rights were similar to the English Bill of Rights and included: freedom of speech, religion, and press; the right to assemble peaceably; the right to trial by jury; and freedom from arbitrary search and seizure of persons or property. The U.S. Constitution would be copied and imitated by many countries as they developed democratic governments.

The Declaration of Independence was a statement of the break the British colonies made from their "mother country" and the establishment of the principles of full democracy. It took a seven-year struggle to achieve that break.

# The Declaration of Independence (1776)

The Declaration of Independence contains the main elements of American democratic traditions. It presents a list of abuses committed by the British government and then details the major rights of the people. The document served as a model for many other governments, especially the following section:

> When in the Course of human events it becomes necessary for one people to dissolve the political bands which have connected them with another and to assume among the powers of the earth, the separate and equal station to which the Laws of Nature and of Nature's God entitle them, a decent respect to the opinions of mankind requires that they should declare the causes which impel them to the separation.

> We hold these truths to be self-evident, that all men are created equal, that they are endowed by their Creator with certain unalienable Rights, that among these are Life, Liberty, and the pursuit of Happiness.—That, to secure these rights, governments are instituted among Men, deriving their just powers from the consent of the governed,—That whenever any Form of Government becomes destructive of these ends, it is the Right of the People to alter or to abolish it, and to institute new government, laying its foundation on such principles and organizing its powers in such form, as to them shall seem most likely to effect their Safety and Happiness.

# The Declaration of the Rights of Man (1789)

Adopted in 1789, the Declaration of the Rights of Man embodied the spirit of the French Revolution. Among the most important articles of the document were:

1. Men are born and remain free and equal in rights. Social distinctions may be founded only upon the general good.

2. The aim of all political association is the preservation of the natural and imprescriptible rights of man. These rights are liberty, property, security, and resistance to oppression.

3. The principle of all sovereignty resides essentially in the nation. No body nor individual may exercise any authority which does not proceed directly from the nation.

4. Liberty consists in the freedom to do everything which injures no one else; hence the exercise of the natural rights of each man has no limits except those which assure to the other members of the society the enjoyment of the same rights. These limits can only be determined by law.

5. Law can only prohibit such actions as are hurtful to society. Nothing may be prevented which is not forbidden by law, and no one may be forced to do anything not provided for by law.

6. Law is the expression of the general will. Every citizen has a right to participate personally, or through his representative, in its foundation. It must be the same for all, whether it protects or punishes. All citizens, being equal in the eyes of the law, are equally eligible to all dignities and to all public positions and occupations, according to their abilities, and without distinction except that of their virtues and talents.

*The French Revolution*
In 1789, soon after the end of the American Revolution, a revolution in France overthrew the monarchy. The aims of the French Revolution were more ambitious than those of the American rebellion. Leaders of the revolution sought to impose a full democracy and to destroy the traditional social order. Although France was declared a republic in 1792, the revolution became more violent and extreme until a new dictatorship emerged under Napoleon Bonaparte. However, even though France was an empire from 1799 to 1815 under Napoleon, it still played an important role in spreading democratic ideals.

Like the American revolutionaries, the French developed a declaration of the rights and freedoms of the people. Known as the Declaration of the Rights of Man (1789), the document echoed the main themes of the Declaration of Independence. However, while the Declaration of Independence was based on Locke's premise of limited government, the Declaration of the Rights of Man was based more on Rousseau's notion of the common good. Ironically, France exported the political sentiments of democracy even as it conquered areas of Europe under Napoleon. Countries such as the Netherlands established democratic institutions under French rule (although they were limited democracies). Many European states also adopted the French legal system, which provided greater rights and freedoms than the traditional systems developed under the European monarchies. In addition, even in France, where the monarchy was reestablished in 1815, the government became a constitutional monarchy with power split between the king and a parliament (although suffrage was limited to the elites).

## EMPIRES AND DEMOCRACY
World history of the nineteenth and twentieth centuries was marked by the effort of some countries to establish empires, while other territories sought to establish themselves as free and independent nations. Many of the colonial powers transplanted democratic institutions and traditions as they conquered new territories. For instance, the countries of Canada, Australia, India, and New Zealand developed into democratic states based on the governmental system of their colonial ruler, Great Britain. Even as colonies, these and other areas had limited democratic systems that included the right to develop legislatures and local self-government.

However, colonialism was mainly an antidemocratic force in the world. Many peoples who had democratic systems in place were conquered and subjugated by the empires of the nineteenth and twentieth centuries. For instance, many Native American tribes, including the Iroquois, had a system of limited democracy, but these systems were destroyed as the people lost their territory to British and American settlers. Furthermore, colonial systems did not allow people in the colonies to vote in national elections. For example, citizens in France could vote on the national president and legislature, but citizens in the colonies could not.

*The World Wars*
World War I (1914–1918) resulted in international efforts to promote full democracy. The Treaty of Versailles (1919), which formally ended the war, created a number of new countries from existing empires in Europe and around the world, and abolished several monarchies, including those in Germany, Austria, and Russia, as a result of the conflict. New democracies with very far-ranging constitutions were established in Germany and other states. In established democracies such as the United States, France, and Great Britain, suffrage was extended to new groups, including women.

Unfortunately many of these countries soon reverted to a new form of tyranny known as fascism. Fascism was a political system based on dictatorship and militarism. In Russia, the monarchy was replaced by an antidemocratic political and economic system known as communism. Communism was an authoritarian system in which the government controlled all economic activity. In Italy, fascists seized power in 1922 when they took over Rome. In Germany, Adolf Hitler (1889–1945) and the Nazi Party gained power by manipulating the political system. By the 1930s, many of the states that had emerged from World War I as democracies had reverted to dictatorships. One result of this trend was the outbreak of World War II as these dictatorships endeavored to expand their territory by conquering neighboring states or establishing new colonies. For instance, in 1939, Germany and Russia invaded Poland and divided the country.

At the end of World War II, the international community again tried to promote democracy. Led by the United States, a variety of institutions and programs were established to foster democracy. By the late 1940s, most of the nations of Western Europe could be considered full democracies. Former fascist countries such as Germany, Italy, and Japan established democratic forms of government, while former colonies, such as India, were granted independence and became democratic countries. Other former colonies underwent difficult transitions to independence that often resulted in the rise of dictatorships, as was the case in the Democratic Republic of the Congo (Zaire), Indonesia, and Uganda.

*The Cold War*

From 1945 until 1989, the United States and the Soviet Union were engaged in a struggle for world domination. Each superpower tried to prevent the other side from acquiring more allies and supporters. During the superpower struggle, the United States undermined some democratic regimes for fear that those countries would support the Soviet Union. At the same time, the United States was the main proponent of world democracy. The United States also became a full democracy, as efforts to promote civil rights in the 1950s and 1960s led to new laws and constitutional amendments that ended official legal racial discrimination in education, politics, economics, and society in the United States. The end of the Cold War ushered in a dramatic rise in the number of democratic countries in the world, but it also led to new questions about what constituted a full democracy and the role of economics in democratic countries.

# Democracy in Practice

**3**

EFFORTS TO ESTABLISH DEMOCRATIC governments have led to the creation of different forms of political systems. Since most philosophers and politicians agreed that direct democracy could not work on a large scale, the central question became how to create a representative democracy that provided the most freedom and equality for a country's citizens. Over the past three centuries many different models were developed, but only a few emerged as workable and popularly accepted ways to organize representative democracies. Even those systems, such as the United States', that have survived for hundreds of years continue to evolve and reform themselves in order to extend the privileges and scope of democracy.

## THE DISTRIBUTION OF POWER IN DEMOCRATIC SYSTEMS

The main issues that differentiate contemporary democratic governments revolve around how the systems distribute political power. Most states have a bicameral legislature. This means that the legislature consists of two chambers. Usually this includes an upper chamber that has certain powers and a second, or lower, chamber with other responsibilities. In the United States, the Senate is the upper chamber and the House of Representatives is the lower chamber. In the United Kingdom, the House of Lords is the upper chamber and the House of Commons is the lower chamber.

The two-chamber system creates a separation of legislative powers that guards against the tyranny of the majority. In addition, in cases such as the U.S. Senate or the German upper house, the Bundesrat, the upper chamber gives states an important role in determining policy. For example, each state in the United States elects two senators who represent the state as a whole. In the House, the number of representatives is based on population, with those representatives responsible to their individual districts. In Germany and Canada, the interests of the states are even more directly represented since the regional governments choose the representatives to the upper chambers.

### Unitary Systems

On another level, the question is how best to share power among national, regional, and local governments. Political systems in which the national government has all, or most, of the power are known as unitary systems. Unitary systems are common in small countries and in those nations that have a history of a strong central government. Many European countries have unitary systems, including France, the United Kingdom, and Hungary. The unitary system remains the most common way to distribute power in the world today.

Unitary systems allow the central government to make most major decisions and laws and therefore ensure uniformity across communities in issues such as education, taxation, and social programs. Critics argue that unitary governments limit democracy because citizens have little control over decisions made about their local issues. In addition, national governments can be remote and unappreciative of factors in local issues.

Nondemocratic governments typically are arranged as unitary systems. Most tyrannical governments have used unitary systems because they allow dictators to concentrate power in their own hands and try to prevent the rise of rivals. In the contemporary world, all of the remaining nondemocratic governments are unitary. This is a factor that critics of unitary systems point out: that if this type of arrangement is most favored by tyrannical regimes, then it must have structural flaws that undermine the democratic processes. Tyrannical regimes use unitary systems to concentrate power and prevent the emergence of alternative ideas or potential leaders. For instance, in a unitary system, local governments derive their existence from the central government. As a result, the national government could abolish local governments or redraw boundaries or change the way it operates with little recourse from the localities.

## Confederations

A political arrangement in which all, or most, of the power is given to regional or local governments is known as a confederation. In confederations, the national government derives its power and responsibility from the regional bodies that can reform or change the central government at will. Confederations work best in small nations or in those countries in which there are deep cultural and societal differences between regions. Within confederations the regional governments are only loosely bound to the central or national government. Confederations allow for the highest degree of local autonomy and control. Like direct democracy, confederations may in principle be the best way to organize governments, but in practice confederations are difficult to govern because of the size of modern countries. One common trend in confederations is that they often break apart as the regions seek independence. For instance, this was the case in the former Yugoslav confederation that broke into Serbia, Montenegro, Bosnia, Croatia, Slovenia, and Macedonia in the 1990s. Confederations are most common in the contemporary world as ways to delegate power in international organizations such as the United Nations and the European Union.

The first official governmental system of the United States was a confederation, based on the Articles of Confederation. However, this government exemplified another trend in confederations. Because of its weak power, under the Articles of Confederation, the national government was unable to respond to problems that faced the new nation. Consequently, instead of breaking apart, the American confederation evolved into a different form of political arrangement in which there was power-sharing between the national government and the governments of the country's regions.

## Federalism

The third way to arrange power between states and the national government is through federalism. Federal systems create some degree of shared power between the regional and national governments. Usually the areas of responsibility and power of the different levels

# The Australian Constitution (1900): Differences between the House and Senate

One common feature for many bicameral legislatures (legislatures that consist of two chambers) is that bills on taxation or appropriations must originate in the lower house. In Australia, as in the United States, Canada, and Germany, any proposed measure on government spending must be passed in the lower chamber and then sent to the upper chamber for ratification.

According to Article 53 of the Australian Constitution, there are also limitations on the ability of the Senate to modify financial legislation:

> Article 53: Proposed laws appropriating revenue or moneys, or imposing taxation, shall not originate in the Senate. But a proposed law shall not be taken to appropriate revenue or moneys, or to impose taxation, by reason only of its containing provisions for the imposition or appropriation of fines or other pecuniary penalties, or for the demand or payment or appropriation of fees for licences, or fees for services under the proposed law.
>
> The Senate may not amend proposed laws imposing taxation, or proposed laws appropriating revenue or moneys for the ordinary annual services of the Government.

The Senate may not amend any proposed law so as to increase any proposed charge or burden on the people.

The Senate may at any stage return to the House of Representatives any proposed law which the Senate may not amend, requesting, by message, the omission or amendment of any items or provisions therein. And the House of Representatives may, if it thinks fit, make any of such omissions or amendments, with or without modifications.

Except as provided in this section, the Senate shall have equal power with the House of Representatives in respect of all proposed laws.

of government are defined through a social contract such as a constitution. Usually power and authority are distributed by dividing areas of responsibility. For instance, the national government may be responsible for defending the country or conducting international diplomacy, while the regional governments may be responsible for education or public safety. Many federal systems actually divide governmental power and responsibility into three levels: national, state, and local. This type of system is present in today's most prominent federal systems, including the United States, Germany, and Canada. These countries all have traditions in which regional governments have substantial autonomy and power.

Federalism combines many of the positive attributes of both unitary systems and confederations. Like unitary systems, federal arrangements allow for a strong central government that keeps the country united and can handle major crises such as war or natural disaster. Like confederations, the federal systems also enable local and regional authorities to decide what is best for their areas based on the wants and needs of their citizens. Hence, federalism enhances democracy because it decentralizes policy- and decision-making. In addition, more layers of government expand the opportunities for people to participate in the political process. Federal systems also provide a way to allow regions to maintain their individual cultural and societal differences but remain part of a larger country. Many of the world's largest democracies, especially those with the greatest degree of ethnic, religious, and linguistic diversification, such as Brazil and India, use federal systems.

## THE PARLIAMENTARY SYSTEM

In addition to dividing power between the national and regional governments, countries have to assign and distribute power within the central government itself. Most countries have implemented Montesquieu's concept of a separation of powers to ensure that one branch of government does not become all-powerful. Two main systems of dividing political power within democratic governments have emerged. The first is the model based on the British Parliament, and the second is the model used by the United States. The major difference between the two models centers around the amount of power given to the executive branch of the government. Both divide their

Many democracies have modeled their form of government on the British parliamentary system. Shown here is an aerial view of the state Opening of Parliament ceremony in the House of Lords.

# The Articles of Confederation (1777)

The Articles of Confederation served as the basis for the first government of the United States. They were adopted in 1777 and came into
force in 1781. The articles gave each state a high degree of power and
provided the national government only limited authority. Among the
significant articles from the document are:

> Article II: Each state retains its sovereignty, freedom, and
> independence, and every power, jurisdiction, and right, which
> is not by this Confederation expressly delegated to the United
> States, in Congress assembled.

> Article III: The said States hereby severally enter into a firm
> league of friendship with each other, for their common
> defense, the security of their liberties, and their mutual and
> general welfare, binding themselves to assist each other,
> against all force offered to, or attacks made upon them, or
> any of them, on account of religion, sovereignty, trade, or any
> other pretense whatever.

> Article V: For the most convenient management of the general
> interests of the United States, delegates shall be annually
> appointed in such manner as the legislatures of each State shall
> direct, to meet in Congress on the first Monday in November,
> in every year, with a power reserved to each State to recall its
> delegates, or any of them, at any time within the year, and to
> send others in their stead for the remainder of the year.

> No State shall be represented in Congress by less than two,
> nor more than seven members; and no person shall be capable
> of being a delegate for more than three years in any term of

six years; nor shall any person, being a delegate, be capable of holding any office under the United States, for which he, or another for his benefit, receives any salary, fees or emolument of any kind.

Each State shall maintain its own delegates in a meeting of the States, and while they act as members of the committee of the States.

In determining questions in the United States in Congress assembled, each State shall have one vote.

Freedom of speech and debate in Congress shall not be impeached or questioned in any court or place out of Congress, and the members of Congress shall be protected in their persons from arrests or imprisonments, during the time of their going to and from, and attendance on Congress, except for treason, felony, or breach of the peace.

# Germany's Constitution and No-Confidence Motions

Articles 67 and 68 of Germany's Constitution, known as the Basic Law, describe how no-confidence votes work in that country (in Germany, the prime minister is known as the Federal Chancellor):

Article 67 (Constructive vote of no confidence)

(1) The Bundestag can express its lack of confidence in the Federal Chancellor only by electing a successor by the majority of its members and by requesting the Federal President to dismiss the Federal Chancellor. The Federal President must comply with the request and appoint the person elected.

(2) Forty-eight hours must elapse between the motion and the election.

Article 68 (Vote of confidence, dissolution of the Bundestag)

(1) If a motion of the Federal Chancellor for a vote of no confidence is not assented to by the majority of the members of the Bundestag, the Federal President may, upon proposal of the Federal Chancellor, dissolve the Bundestag within twenty-one days. The right to dissolve lapses as soon as the Bundestag by the majority of its members elects another Federal Chancellor.

(2) Forty-eight hours must elapse between the motion and the vote thereon.

branches of government into the three main categories of executive, legislative, and judicial.

The British system has become the most widely copied form of representative democracy. It is commonly known as the parliamentary, or Westminster (the name of the place where the British Parliament meets), system. The Westminster system evolved over hundreds of years as Parliament slowly took power away from the British monarchs. One result is that Parliament operated for many years, until the 1700s, with an external executive branch—the monarchy. During this time, it was the monarchy that controlled the bureaucracy, the military, and the country's diplomacy. Parliament's role was to advise the monarchy and to deliberate on tax and revenue issues. Consequently, the country has historically had a very strong and powerful executive branch, even though that executive was nondemocratic for much of its history.

### Combined Executive and Legislative Branches

In the parliamentary system there is no clear separation between the executive and legislative branches. Instead, the leaders of the executive branch, including the head of the government, the prime minister, and other cabinet officials, are usually members of the legislature. Rather than directly elect the prime minister, voters elect members to parliament, and the leader of the largest group in parliament becomes the chief executive. The prime minister then appoints other members of parliament to run the ministries or cabinet offices. Hence, the majority group in parliament is responsible for both enacting and implementing laws and policies (unlike other systems in which the legislature creates and passes laws, while the executive branch enforces the law). A group needs a majority of the seats in parliament in order to form a government. Sometimes a single party cannot muster that majority and must ask other parties to join it. The result is known as a coalition government, or one in which at least two different parties form the cabinet.

The parliamentary system has several advantages and disadvantages. Since the government always has a majority in parliament, its plans and policies are always approved, except under extraordinary circumstances. This means that parliamentary systems tend to be more efficient and flexible in creating and implementing policies. If at any given point the government cannot secure a majority, a no-confidence vote can be taken. If a majority of members of parliament vote against the government in a no-confidence vote, the government must resign and new elections are held. The prime minister can also usually dissolve parliament and call for new elections if he or she deems it necessary (this might occur in response to a crisis within the government or a national emergency). Because of the ability of the government to be dissolved at any point, parliamentary systems are often criticized for being unstable. For instance, there have been almost sixty different governments in Italy since World War II.

## THE U.S. PRESIDENTIAL SYSTEM

With the Treaty of Paris (1783), the United States became an independent nation. In order to govern the new country, a confederation of the states came into force in 1781. Under the Articles of Confederation, the new government had a one-chamber, or unicameral, legislature, known as Congress, in which all of the states had equal representation. The government epitomized the principles of limited government based on a social contract. At the state and local levels, there was a greater degree of freedom and democracy as several states adopted state constitutions that guaranteed freedoms such as religion and speech, while other states began to abolish slavery.

*Checks and Balances*

The Articles of Confederation ultimately did not work because Congress did not have the power to tax, and the passage of legislation required a two-thirds majority vote (amending the articles required a unanimous vote). The articles were replaced in 1789 with the present Constitution, which established a presidential system. The new organization of government was based on a separation of powers.

The legislative and executive branches were divided (unlike parliamentary systems), and there was also a separate judicial branch. This system was designed to keep any one branch of government from becoming all-powerful. This concept is known as the system of checks and balances, since the different branches both "check" and "balance" one another. For instance, the executive can veto legislation, but the legislature often has the ability to overturn a veto through a supermajority vote (a majority of three-quarters or more).

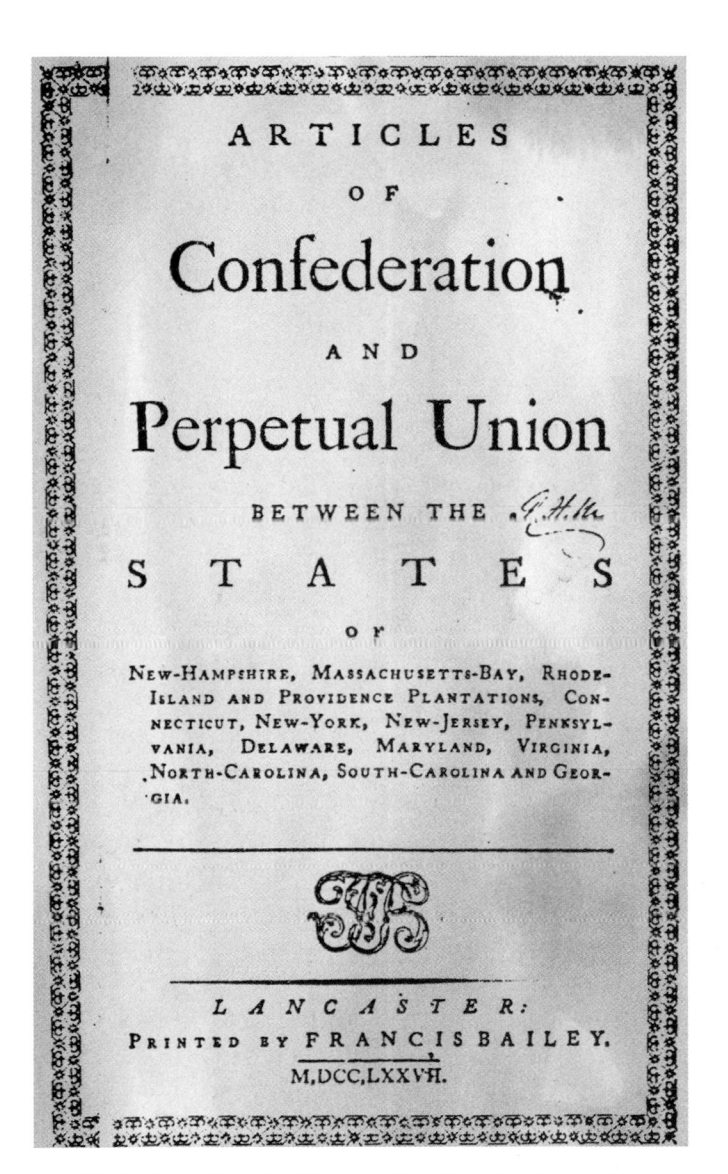

**This is a facsimile of the title page of the first printed copy of the Articles of Confederation (1777).**

*Advantages and Disadvantages of Presidential Systems*

The American system became the model for other presidential forms of government. In addition to the separation of powers, another significant feature of presidential systems is that the president, or executive, is directly elected by the people, whereas a prime minister is elected by other members of parliament. This gives the president a greater degree of legitimacy and authority before the population, since the executive has a direct mandate from the people (the United States and a few other countries do not directly elect the president, an issue discussed in Chapter 5). Because the president is elected separately from the legislature, that body can usually remove, or impeach, the chief executive because of presidential misconduct. The result is that presidential systems generally are more stable than parliamentary governments.

This stability is not always good, as the inability to remove a bad chief executive can cause continuing problems for the country. Furthermore, in many presidential systems, chief executives have used their office to acquire tyrannical powers and even overturn democracy. For instance, presidents have used military force to disband legislatures and assume complete control of the government in countries such as Ecuador, Haiti, and Nigeria.

Proponents of presidential systems argue that they can respond more quickly to disasters or national emergencies. However, often the ability of the chief executive to act is dependent upon support from the legislature. If the legislature and the chief executive are of different political parties, the result can be an inability to take action (a condition known as gridlock) as both sides try to gain political advantage by making the other party look bad in the eyes of voters. People who favor limited government do not see gridlock as a problem but as an asset of presidential systems, because the condition limits the ability of the government to expand its power or scope. Such sentiments were common among the framers of the U.S. Constitution and remain popular with political conservatives.

## SEMI-PRESIDENTIAL SYSTEMS

A few countries have systems that combine parliamentary and presidential democracies. One of the best known semi-presidential systems is France. In France, the legislature elects a prime minister as do all parliamentary systems, but there is also a president who is directly elected by the people.

The result is a system in which the executive branch is divided between a cabinet led by the prime minister and the office of the presidency.

One of the main disadvantages of the French system is that it is possible to have a president from one political party and a prime minister from a different party. This situation is known as cohabitation. The result of cohabitation is usually gridlock and an unofficial division of power between the two executives in which the president concentrates on foreign policy while the prime minister is in charge of domestic issues.

# 4

■ ■ ■ Political and Economic Development

AT THE CORE OF DEMOCRATIC SYSTEMS is the ideal of liberty. Democracy has traditionally granted people the greatest degree of personal freedom. This has included not only political liberty, but also substantial social and economic freedom. For instance, among the reasons given for the American Revolution and the formation of the subsequent republic was the ability to promote social equality and economic opportunity. In addition, many constitutions enshrine these twin principles as the basis for a country's social contract between its people and the government. Many political philosophers even assert that the main purposes of government are to ensure social equity and to protect economic gains. In spite of the relationship between democracy and social and economic freedom, there continues to be considerable debate over whether modern democracies are truly able to provide equal opportunities to all citizens. This chapter examines the broad philosophical concepts that guide democracies and the large problems faced when trying to ensure equality.

## INDIVIDUALISM AND THE COMMON GOOD
Modern democratic governments are an effort to reconcile two opposites: Locke's notion of individual rights and Rousseau's belief in government for the common good. Under Locke's view of democracy, governments exist only to protect the property and rights of individuals.

Locke believed that people were born with natural rights, known as civil liberties, the government could not take away. If a government tried to infringe on the civil liberties of its citizens, then people had an inherent right to revolt. Locke believed that a government had a right to exist only through the collective consent of its citizens.

Locke's conceptualization portrays government, even a democratic one, as something intrusive: an institution that must be contained and vigorously watched lest it attempt to infringe on the rights of its citizens and take away the power and authority that belonged first to the citizenry. For instance, Locke believed that if people acquired or owned land, then the government could only take that property away under extraordinary circumstances (such as failure to pay taxes or in a national emergency—in which case the government would have to compensate the landowner). In another example, if he had lived in modern times, Locke would most likely argue that all citizens should be taxed at the same rate.

Rousseau saw democratic government as a potential force for good. The French philosopher believed that democracies would be able to address some of the ills and problems of society in order to improve the lives of its citizenry. Rousseau argued that a democratic government had a justified ability to violate some of the individual rights of its citizens if the result improved the lives of others. He believed that the democratic process provided a means for different groups to discuss and debate needs. From this interaction, the otherwise selfish interests of the groups would be eroded and a consensus of the general will of the people would emerge. For example, Rousseau would argue that in contemporary times, the wealthier citizens would be willing to pay a higher tax rate in order to help the poor since such a process would ultimately benefit the country as a whole.

The conflict between the ideas of Locke and Rousseau continues to occur in modern democratic countries. Democratic governments have to balance the rights and privileges of the individual with the common good. For instance, in the United States, the Fourth Amendment to the Constitution provides individuals with protections against unreasonable search and seizure of property. This means that government agents such as the police must have a warrant in order to search someone's property. If the police conduct a search without a warrant, evidence seized may be thrown out by a court. In this instance, the right of the individual to be safe from unnecessary or illegal searches outweighs the societal need to prevent crimes or to apprehend criminals.

# John Locke and Government by Consent

John Locke's *Second Treatise of Government* (1690) contains Locke's main political philosophies and details how the author envisioned government by consent. In this passage Locke explains his notion of how people grant their consent to the government to be governed:

Section 119: Every man being, as has been shewed [showed], naturally free, and nothing being able to put him into subjection to any earthly power, but only his own consent; it is to be considered, what shall be understood to be a sufficient declaration of a man's consent, to make him subject to the laws of any government. There is a common distinction of an express and a tacit consent, which will concern our present case. Nobody doubts but an express consent, of any man entering into any society, makes him a perfect member of that society, a subject of that government. The difficulty is, what ought to be looked upon as a tacit consent, and how far it binds, i.e. how far any one shall be looked on to have consented, and thereby submitted to any government, where he has made no expressions of it at all. And to this I say, that every man, that hath any possessions, or enjoyment, of any part of the dominions of any government, doth thereby give his tacit consent, and is as far forth obliged to obedience to the laws of that government, during such enjoyment, as any one under it; whether this his possession be of land, to him and his heirs for ever, or a lodging only for a week; or whether it be barely travelling freely on the highway; and in effect, it reaches as far as the very being of any one within the territories of that government.

British philosopher John Locke (1632–1704) believed that government existed solely to protect the rights of individuals.

## ELITISM VERSUS PLURALISM

All societies, even those with democratic governments, have citizens who are more powerful than others. That power inequality may be the result of economic factors, or it could be based on race, ethnicity, religion, or even political tradition. Efforts to protect the rights of individuals may sometimes exacerbate these inequities by preserving unequal economic or social systems. However, by trying to protect the rights of all individuals, class or power distinctions may be overcome. At the same time, attempts to promote the general will could lead to greater social equilibrium, or they could undermine the status of minority groups if the common good is defined in such a way as to protect the existing social order. Scholars who study democracy have developed two main ways to define the level of equality of societies: elitism and pluralism. These academic approaches are descriptive theories of how some democracies operate in practice.

*Elitism*

Elitism, sometimes referred to as class theory, asserts that most societies are divided by class and that upper-class elites dominate governments, even democratic ones. Small groups of the rich, including business and social leaders and prominent citizens, constitute these elites. In many developed democracies in North America and Europe, elites are often associated with particular races, especially Caucasians; male gender; and religion. In addition, elites often have a similar educational or social background. In the United States, elites often are graduates of Ivy League colleges such as Harvard University or Yale University. They often belong to prominent families such as the Bushes or the Kennedys.

Elitism holds that wealth, not individual rights or democracy, is the real cornerstone of political power. This wealth could include stocks, property, monetary resources, and/or ownership of companies and corporations. Even in democracies, wealth tends to be concentrated among a small percentage of the population. For instance, in the United States, the richest one percent of the population controls one-third of the country's wealth, and the richest 10 percent control more than 50 percent of American wealth.

The elites use their wealth to dominate policy-making and to ensure that other groups are prevented from influencing representative governments. They are better able to contribute to political causes and campaigns. In the United States, candidates for the House of

Representatives spent an average of $1 million on their campaigns in 2004, while Senate campaigns cost an average of $2 million. This highlights the importance of wealthy donors for those who seek elected office. In addition, elites can provide funding for media campaigns on certain issues and raise public awareness of their concerns.

Elites do not overtly control the government. There can be duly constituted elections, and representatives often come from a cross-section of society. However, elites are able to manipulate the policy process through special access to representatives and undue influence on the media because of their wealth. Central to class theory is the notion that it does not matter which political party is in power because, as a result of their wealth, the same elites are always able to influence the government.

*Pluralism*

The pluralism theory of democracy contends that groups within a society compete for power and influence and this competition prevents any one group from dominating the government for long periods of time. Pluralism asserts that no single elite can hold political power for extended periods because other groups would join together to undermine the elite. Proponents of pluralism argue that a range of factors keeps any single group from exerting undue influence in democratic politics. For example, the separation of powers and the system of checks and balances common in most presidential democracies reinforce the inability of elites to dominate the government. In addition, systems that have multiple political parties dilute the influence of any one group. Furthermore, most full democracies have rules and regulations that limit the ability of groups to dominate a country's media.

Instead of domination, pluralism holds that groups are forced to bargain and compromise to gain their objectives. Even if a group can gain governmental dominance for a period, over time its compromises will reduce its power and open the political system. Also, because of the need to bargain, interest groups often have to form coalitions with other groups in order to achieve their objectives. The framers of the U.S. Constitution even believed that the multitude of interests would help promote a healthy democracy by diffusing political power. In many modern democracies, a wide range of interest groups seek to promote either broad or specific issues. In the United States, examples of

# Spending in the 2004 U.S. Presidential Election

The amount of money spent on American presidential campaigns has grown dramatically in the past few decades. Campaign contributions in 2004 set new records. The high level of money involved in the campaigns reinforces the main arguments of elite theory for many people because of the sheer volume of money needed to be elected. According to preliminary reports published by the Federal Election Commission about the 2004 presidential campaign, through August of that year candidates had raised more than $661.9 million. The breakdown of individual candidates was:

**Republican Party**
George W. Bush                   $258,939,099

**Republican Total**             $258,939,099

## Democratic Party

| | |
|---|---|
| Wesley Clark | $25,073,530 |
| Howard Dean | $51,126,828 |
| John Edwards | $29,206,170 |
| Richard Gephardt | $21,203,139 |
| John Kerry | $233,985,144 |
| Dennis Kucinich | $10,669,287 |
| Lyndon LaRouche | $9,606,640 |
| Joseph Lieberman | $18,536,930 |
| Carol Moseley Braun | $582,547 |
| Al Sharpton | $589,866 |
| **Democratic Total** | **$400,580,081** |

## Other

| | |
|---|---|
| Ralph Nader | $2,373,338 |

such groups include: business organizations such as the Chamber of Commerce and the National Retailers Association; environmental groups such as the Sierra Club and Greenpeace; civil rights groups such as the National Organization for Women (NOW) and the National Association for the Advancement of Colored People (NAACP); and special, or single, interest groups such as the National Rifle Association (NRA) and Mothers Against Drunk Driving (MADD).

*Hyperpluralism*

The development of interest groups has led many to argue that the competition for influence is now out of control in some full democracies. Hyperpluralism refers to a condition in which the competition between groups is so intense that representatives cannot craft policies. Hyperpluralism results when groups are able to push their interests ahead of the common good. Instead of bargaining, groups force the adoption of their preferred policies. The difference between elitism and hyperpluralism is that while elites tend to be a unified group, hyperpluralism results in a large number of groups with varying amounts of power. Another problem that arises with hyperpluralism is that disadvantaged groups such as the poor or minorities are often excluded from powerful interest groups or face significant hurdles to creating and maintaining these groups.

## FREE MARKET DEMOCRACY

Many democratic countries continue to experience broad inequalities in wealth and status. Often this is the result of the power and influence of elites. In other cases, economic factors can create great differences between those at the top of a society and those at the bottom. Locke's emphasis on the individual influenced later democratic thinkers such as James Madison (1751–1836) and Thomas Jefferson, who both tried to combine the free market economic principles of Adam Smith (1723–1790) with the political concepts of Locke. The result was free market democracy. Those who embrace this idea argue that self-interest and competition drive economic interactions and that the main role of the government is to protect wealth and property, not regulate the economy. This notion of negative freedom (or freedom from government) is one of the main political underpinnings of the U.S. democratic system. Many people argue that negative freedom and civil liberties are one and the same.

e feature of democracies is interest groups focused on specific government policies. In 2003, Greenpeace activists
ged a protest against genetic food engineering in a nonorganic corn field in the Zaragoza region of Spain.

# Adam Smith and Free Market Economics

Scottish economist Adam Smith is regarded as the father of free market economics. His 1776 book, *On the Wealth of Nations,* remains one of the most read books on international economics. Here, Smith explains how self-interest drives economic interactions:

> In almost every other race of animals each individual, when it is grown up to maturity, is entirely independent, and in its natural state has occasion for the assistance of no other living creature. But man has almost constant occasion for the help of his brethren, and it is in vain for him to expect it from their benevolence only. He will be more likely to prevail if he can interest their self-love in his favor, and show them that it is for their own advantage to do for him what he requires of them. Whoever offers to another a bargain of any kind, proposes to do this. Give me that which I want, and you shall have this which you want, is the meaning of every such offer; and it is in this manner that we obtain from one another the far greater part of those good offices which we stand in need of. It is not from the benevolence of the butcher, the brewer, or the baker that we expect our dinner, but from their regard to their own interest. We address ourselves, not to their humanity but to their self-love, and never talk to them of our own necessities but of their advantages. Nobody but a beggar chooses to depend chiefly upon the benevolence of his fellow citizens. Even a beggar does not depend upon it entirely. The charity of well-disposed people, indeed, supplies him with the whole fund of his subsistence. But though this principle ultimately provides him with all the necessaries of life which

he has occasion for, it neither does nor can provide him with them as he has occasion for them. The greater part of his occasional wants are supplied in the same manner as those of other people, by treaty, by barter, and by purchase. With the money which one man gives him he purchases food. The old clothes which another bestows upon him he exchanges for other old clothes which suit him better, or for lodging, or for food, or for money, with which he can buy either food, clothes, or lodging, as he has occasion.

Citizens in a full democracy are free to protest policies they deplore. These fake gravestones were placed in Trafalgar Square, London, to protest the arms policies of its government, and those of most of the other great powers.

Free market democracy holds that government should be as limited as feasible and that most areas of policy, including the economy, health care, and social services, should be left to the private market. For instance, instead of government aid programs, free market democracy would rely more on charity and philanthropy to address social problems. Proponents of this philosophy believe that the private sector is almost always more efficient than government services. Finally, free market democracy also contends that competition will prevent the dominance of elites.

*Inequality and the Free Market*
Opponents of free market democracy promote positive freedom (freedom to accomplish or to reach one's full potential). They argue that government has an important role to play in helping people and, therefore, providing for the common good. For instance, adherents of free market democracy accept that economies sometimes have high unemployment. They prefer job growth that results from changes in the economy rather than from government action. On the other hand, people who advocate positive freedom want the government to implement measures to stimulate the economy and, perhaps, even provide jobs for citizens.

Without government oversight of the economy, elites within society are able to exploit their wealth and power to benefit themselves at the expense of the middle-class and poor. Over time this will distort the free market and create artificial barriers to nonelite groups. In addition, large corporations can become very powerful, especially in small- or medium-sized countries. They can exert undue pressure on governments to adopt policies that benefit these corporations to the detriment of the common good.

As a result, modern democratic countries, including the United States, have adopted mixed economic systems that combine elements of the free market and government regulation. For instance, governments establish minimum wages and rules and regulations on working conditions, and monitor the production and sale of drugs and foodstuffs. Governments also provide health, education, and retirement programs for their citizens. One of the determinants for a modern full democracy is whether the government can ensure the basic needs and services for its citizens. Some countries, such as the United States, rely more on the private sector to provide many services, while most

European states and Canada have the government oversee major social programs. Many countries trying to establish democratic systems have a difficult time acquiring the resources necessary to meet the needs of their citizens. This often causes discontent with even democratically elected governments. Furthermore, even in advanced full democracies such as the United States, cultural and political barriers often perpetuate inequalities and discrimination.

# 5
## Democracy in Perspective ■ ■ ▬

MODERN DEMOCRATIC SYSTEMS EVOLVED as a way to lessen the inequalities of societies and to provide all citizens with equal political power. However, even in contemporary, advanced, full democracies, inequities persist. In some cases, such disparities in wealth, political power, and social standing are the result of a country's political culture—the traditions, values, and principles that form the basis of a nation's political system. In other cases, economic factors can contribute to inequality, as can racial, ethnic, or religious discrimination. Even democratic systems are not able to erase all types of inequality, but countries must make all reasonable efforts to eliminate these problems in order to be full democracies.

## MAJORITY RULE AND MINORITY RIGHTS
Democracies have to balance majority rule with minority rights. Democratic governments have to craft policies that reflect the will and interests of the majority of the population but that do not alienate or marginalize minority groups. Even in a full democracy the danger of the tyranny of the majority remains very real. Central to the potential abuse of the minority is the fact that in a democracy, the majority can always outvote the minority. This results in elections or policies that are perceived of as "fair" or legitimate by the majority, but since the needs of the minorities are often overlooked, these groups perceive democracy as unfair and the political process as biased against them. This is one

# Language Education Rights in Canada

In order to protect the language rights of minority speakers in Canada, Section 23 of the country's Charter of Rights and Freedoms (1982) mandates that the children of French speakers in majority English areas and of English speakers in majority French areas have to be able to receive an education in their native language. The charter states that provinces have to provide minority language instruction either in formal classes in the provincial school system or by paying for private instruction:

23. (1) Citizens of Canada

(a) whose first language learned and still understood is that of the English or French linguistic minority of the province in which they reside, or

(b) who have received their primary school instruction in Canada in English or French and reside in a province where the language in which they received that instruction is the language of the English or French linguistic minority population of the province, have the right to have their children receive primary and secondary school instruction in that language in that province.

(2) Citizens of Canada of whom any child has received or is receiving primary or secondary school instruction in English or French in Canada, have the right to have all their children receive primary and secondary language instruction in the same language.

(3) The right of citizens of Canada under subsections (1) and (2) to have their children receive primary and secondary school instruction in the language of the English or French linguistic minority population of a province:

(a) applies wherever in the province the number of children of citizens who have such a right is sufficient to warrant the provision to them out of public funds of minority language instruction; and

Democratic governments try to protect the rights of all of their citizens. Two schoolgirls run past political graffiti calling for a French Quebec, rather than a Quebec in which English and French carry equal weight. Though the French are a minority in Canada, they are a majority in the province of Quebec.

(b) includes, where the number of those children so warrants, the right to have them receive that instruction in minority language educational facilities provided out of public funds.

of the main problems with direct democracy; even in representative democracies, the tendency for elected officials is to make the needs and interests of the majority their main priority.

Both federalism and confederalism offer organizational methods to protect minority rights. By giving more power to regional governments, it is possible to provide greater political influence to minority groups if the regions have high populations of these groups. Within a given country, the majority group may make up 70 percent of the population, but within a given region, a minority may dominate. Hence, that group would enjoy the full spectrum of the political process. For example, in Canada, 60 percent of the population speak English, while only 24 percent speak French (the remaining 16 percent speak a variety of indigenous languages, Spanish, and Hindi). However, in the province of Quebec, 80 percent of the people speak French, giving them a majority in their regional government. In addition, minority groups may be able to exert greater political power at the local level in towns and cities.

This effort to maintain a balance between the majority and minority can be especially complicated in countries that have histories of discrimination against specific groups. Often the discrimination faced by minority groups does not exist at an official level; in other words, the laws and policies of a government are not technically discriminatory. However, groups are still at a disadvantage because of cultural or societal factors that are difficult for governments to overcome through official actions. In other cases, minority groups have enjoyed special or privileged positions in society, often forming part of governing elites, and the effort to democratize a country may involve redistributing privileges away from these groups.

## POLITICAL DISCRIMINATION

Political discrimination existed in all countries throughout most of history. Even those countries considered full democracies today have long histories of discrimination. No country allowed all women full access to political power or suffrage until the late 1800s. In addition, many countries had laws that prevented minority groups from voting or holding office. As noted in earlier chapters, democracies were initially dominated by elites. Within the limited democracies of ancient Athens, and even in the early United States, elites feared that majority rule would lead to chaos and anarchy. As a result, a variety of impediments were put in place to prevent average citizens from becoming involved in the democratic process.

In the early United States, minority groups, women, and poor whites were excluded from voting. Only about 10 percent of the adult population was eligible to vote or hold elected office. Most elected offices required a certain amount of property or wealth. Of the original thirteen states, only Pennsylvania did not have such requirements. In South Carolina, candidates for the state senate had to have property or wealth equivalent to at least £7,000 (or about $1 million today), while in Maryland, candidates for the governor's office needed wealth equal to £5,000 (more than $700,000 in U.S. dollars today).

In order to spread political rights to all U.S. citizens, a succession of constitutional amendments were passed. For instance, African Americans were not allowed to vote in the South before the end of the Civil War and the passage of the Fifteenth Amendment (1870). In addition, U.S. senators were elected by state legislatures, not the people, until the Seventeenth Amendment (1913), which called for direct elections. The Nineteenth Amendment (1920) gave women the right to vote. Over time, suffrage was gradually extended to all groups in the United States, but even today in other countries there continue to be official restrictions on the ability of some groups to vote or hold office. In many countries in the Middle East, women are excluded from voting or holding political office.

*Unofficial Discrimination*

Often countries pass laws that result in political discrimination, or that limit people's political power, even if the rules or regulations are officially neutral. For instance, if citizens speak a language other than a country's official tongue, they may be unable to read a ballot. In response, many countries now print ballots in multiple languages. In the United States, ballots are printed in approximately twenty different languages, ranging from Spanish and French to Arabic and Mandarin Chinese. The United States used a variety of laws that officially did not discriminate because of race but that had the effect of disenfranchising African Americans. These laws included literacy tests, poll taxes, and grandfather laws— laws that required a person's grandfather to have been eligible to vote in order for that person to be allowed to cast a ballot (since slaves were not allowed to vote, the law effectively disenfranchised the children and grandchildren of former slaves). It was not until the 1960s that most of these laws were overturned or abolished.

In order to safeguard the ability of people to participate in the political process, full democracies must adopt a range of measures to prevent unofficial discrimination. For instance, almost all full democracies now use the Australian ballot. The Australian ballot is one that is secret, and it is prepared, tabulated, and paid for by the government. In the United States, all states have used the Australian ballot since 1888. It provides the best way to make sure that officials cannot retaliate against voters if they cast ballots for candidates opposed to the government. Before the widespread adoption of the Australian ballot, many countries used methods of voting that allowed officials to know how people cast their ballots. Some places used oral voting, while other countries or states used ballots that were different colors, depending on the political party of the particular candidate.

*Voting Systems*
One continuing issue of debate in democracies is the system of voting. Originally, all democracies used a winner-take-all system (sometimes also referred to as first-past-the-post). Under this system, whichever candidate receives the most votes in a district wins the election. If there are three candidates and one receives 40 percent of the vote, another receives 30 percent, and a third receives 30 percent, the winner is the candidate with 40 percent, even though 60 percent of the people voted against that candidate. Countries such as the United States and the United Kingdom use winner-take-all systems, which tend to reinforce the dominance of the majority. For instance, in the United States, parties outside of the two main political groups, the Republicans and Democrats, have had very little electoral success. One result is stability and a limited number of parties. Both the United States and the United Kingdom have been dominated by a two-party system through most of their histories.

On the other hand, an increasing number of countries are utilizing proportional representation in order to expand minority participation in politics. Under proportional representation, vote results are directly proportional to the vote distribution. If a party receives 30 percent of the vote, it receives 30 percent of the representation. This allows parties or candidates who receive smaller percentages

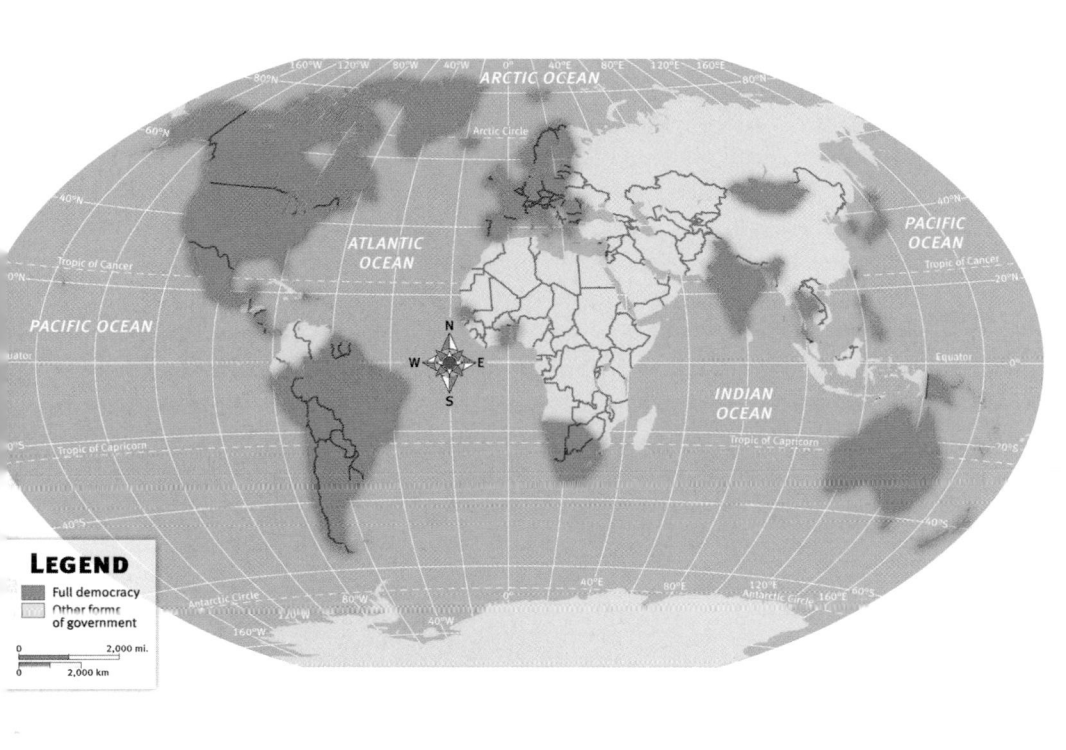

**Democratic Countries**

LEGEND

Full democracy

Other forms
of government

0          2,000 mi.

0          2,000 km

of the votes to have some representation in the government. Most systems that use proportional representation do have a minimum threshold, which means that a party or candidate must receive a minimum percentage of the vote (usually 5 percent) in order to gain representation. Proportional representation allows smaller parties to gain seats in a legislature and, hence, results in greater diversity of opinion and viewpoint. It also allows minority groups a better chance of obtaining representation in government. However, the system also results in a more fragmented government, and many systems that use proportional representation have a high turnover in government.

Ireland and Australia use a special, though complicated, form of proportional representation known as a single-transfer system to ensure minority representation. Under this system, voters rank their preference for candidates or parties by listing them as "one," "two," "three," and so forth. Candidates must meet a predetermined quota of number "one" votes in order to gain a seat. If no one meets the quota, the candidates with the fewest number "one" votes are eliminated and those votes are given to the highest number "two" votes are those who voted for the disqualified number "one" candidates. In the United States, the city of Cambridge, Massachusetts, uses this system in local elections, and several other localities have experimented with the system as a means to improve minority representation.

Countries such as Italy, Israel, and Germany often have to form coalition governments in their parliaments. Since parliamentary systems require a majority of support from the legislature, parties have to form alliances since none of the parties have an outright majority of 50.1 percent of the seats. For instance, in Germany, the government elected in 2002 was formed by a coalition of the Social Democratic Party and the Green Party. The German parliament has 669 seats. The Social Democrats won 251, and the Greens 55, with the rest split between a dozen other parties. Combined, the two parties thus had a plurality. Often coalition governments require three or more parties. This makes governing difficult, as parties can threaten to withdraw from the government and thus force a no-confidence vote, if they do not get their way on policy issues.

Some systems actively seek to include minority representation no matter what the election results. For instance, in Poland, political parties representing ethnic Germans are guaranteed at least two seats in the Polish parliament. Other countries use similar arrangements to ensure that minority groups are never completely shut out of the government. Other systems take the opposite approach and force a candidate always to have an absolute majority. These systems use run-off elections. In these systems, a candidate must have a clear majority of 50.1 percent of the vote. If in the general election no candidate receives a majority, a special election called a run-off occurs in which the top two candidates face each other. France uses this system to elect its president, and in the United States, Louisiana uses this system. Run-offs often mean candidates must appeal to the majority in order to be elected.

## THE ELECTORAL COLLEGE

Presidential elections in the United States provide an example of the manner in which there continue to be limits on full democracy. The United States still uses a system of indirect election for the office of the presidency. The U.S. president is actually elected by a body known as the electoral college. This body is made up of representatives from each of the fifty states. The number of representatives (known as electors) a state has is based on its congressional representation. For instance, Mississippi has four members of the House and two senators, therefore it has six electors. Texas has thirty-two representatives and two senators, thus it has thirty-four electors.

In order to be elected president, a candidate must receive a majority of the electoral vote (or votes from 278 electors). The electoral college is a winner-take-all system. Whichever candidate wins the greatest number of votes in a state receives all of the state's electoral votes (only Maine and Nebraska allow electoral votes to be split between candidates). Electors are chosen by political parties, so if the Republican Party candidate wins a state, Republican electors cast the state's electoral ballots; if a Democratic candidate wins, it is that party that picks the electors. Most states require electors to vote for the party that chose them, but in 1796, 1820, 1948, 1956, 1960, 1968, 1972, 1976, and 1988, electors voted for candidates from different parties because of ideological differences.

Many people assert that the electoral college unfairly benefits states with large populations. A state such as California with fifty-five electoral votes, or Texas, with thirty-four votes, or New York, with thirty-one votes, often receives more campaign attention from candidates running for office since those high state numbers of electoral votes would go a long way toward the total number needed. On the other

# Proportional Representation in Cambridge, Massachusetts

Cambridge uses proportional representation to elect local officials, including the nine-member city council. The Cambridge system is complicated, but it has increased minority representation and allowed small parties to gain seats on the council. It works in the following manner. Voters mark their preference for candidates as "one," "two," "three," and on until they have ranked all of the candidates.

A quota is established for winning candidates based on the number of ballots cast. The quota is decided by taking the total number of ballots cast and dividing it by the number of seats at stake, plus one. Thus, the city council would be nine plus one, or ten. If 20,000 votes were cast, the figure would be 20,000 divided by 10, or 2,000. One is then added to the figure to make the quota, 2,001.

To count the results, first, any candidates in the number one spot who reach the quota automatically win. All the votes that they receive above the 2,001 quota are redistributed to candidates in the number two preference spot. At the same time, any candidate who received fewer than fifty votes is automatically eliminated and his or her votes are redistributed to the number two candidates. In addition, the candidate with the overall lowest vote total is eliminated and his or her votes are redistributed. If someone in the number two spot reaches 2,001, he or she wins a seat. After the votes are redistributed, if no one in the number two spot reaches the quota, the process moves on to the number three spot and begins again, until there are nine winners.

In the United States, if a president wins the majority of the electoral votes, he or she wins the election. In 2000, students at Florida A & M University held a sit-in to protest what they believed were irregularities in the vote count.

# Counting the Electoral College Votes

Section 15 of Chapter 1 of Title 3 of the United States Code defines how the final electoral votes are counted in Congress:

15. Congress shall be in session on the sixth day of January succeeding every meeting of the electors. The Senate and House of Representatives shall meet in the Hall of the House of Representatives at the hour of 1 o'clock in the afternoon on that day, and the President of the Senate shall be their presiding officer. Two tellers shall be previously appointed on the part of the Senate and two on the part of the House of Representatives, to whom shall be handed, as they are opened by the President of the Senate, all the certificates and papers purporting to be certificates of the electoral votes, which certificates and papers shall be opened, presented, and acted upon in the alphabetical order of the States, beginning with the letter A; and said tellers, having then read the same in the presence and hearing of the two Houses, shall make a list of the votes as they shall appear from the said certificates; and the votes having been ascertained and counted according to the rules in this subchapter provided, the result of the same shall be delivered to the President of the Senate, who shall thereupon announce the state of the vote, which announcement shall be deemed a sufficient declaration of the persons, if any, elected President and Vice President of the United States, and, together with a list of the votes, be entered on the Journals of the two Houses.

hand, since all states have a minimum of three electoral votes (equal to the minimum of two senators and one representative), votes in some of the smaller states actually count more. For instance, Alaska, with three electoral votes, gets one vote for about every 185,000 people, while New York has one vote for every 545,000 people.

More significantly, in several presidential elections in U.S. history, the candidate who received the most votes did not win the election because of the electoral college. John Quincy Adams (1824), Rutherford B. Hayes (1876), Benjamin Harrison (1888), and George W. Bush (2000) were all elected president by the electoral college even though each received fewer popular votes than their main opponent. The 2000 election caused a bitter and divisive political battle over recounting ballots in the state of Florida, which in turn led to reforms of how ballots were prepared and printed. It also prompted an increase in the use of electronic voting machines that tend to have lower error rates than machines that use manual ballots. In the election, Bush won 50,461,080 votes while his opponent, incumbent Vice President Al Gore, received 50,994,082 votes, or 533,002 more votes than Bush. However, Bush won thirty states to Gore's twenty (interestingly, Bush won 2,434 counties to Gore's 677, demonstrating that Gore's popularity tended to be in the more highly populated urban areas).

# 6
■ ■■■ Democracy and Other Governments

DEMOCRATIC GOVERNMENTS DO SHARE some characteristics with other political systems. For instance, democracies can be organized as unitary, confederal, or federal systems. The same organizational models can be applied to nondemocratic governments. However, the distribution of power within democratic systems makes them significantly different from other forms of government. By granting the people ultimate power and authority over the political process, democracies provide the best means both to ensure majority rule and to protect minority interests. Because of the involvement of the people, democracies are often more complex and diverse than their nondemocratic counterparts.

## TYPES OF GOVERNMENT

In general, there are three broad ways to categorize a government. One is democracy, which, as discussed, means that a country's citizens control the government and policy process. Ideally, a democratic system serves the interests and needs of its people. At the opposite extreme is tyranny, in which all or most political power is concentrated in the government itself. Often tyrannical governments, such as monarchies or dictatorships, are developed to serve the needs of, or to benefit, the rulers. Hence, one of the main differences between a democracy and a tyrannical government is that the former serves the people and the latter serves the rulers. In addition, a full democracy serves the

Though the United Kingdom is a democracy, its titular head remains Queen Elizabeth. The queen presides over official functions such as this visit to the Honor Guard in Kingston, Jamaica, which took place in 1983.

interests both of the majority and minority groups, and consequently is able to bring its citizens together as a unifying force. On the other hand, tyrannical governments often adopt policies to purposely divide people and to exacerbate differences in order to prevent citizens from joining together to overthrow the government. The final system of government is anarchy. In an anarchical system, there is no central government. Instead politics are marked by chaos. Anarchical political systems are short-lived. Most often anarchy is the result of the collapse of one of the other forms of government. As a result, any comparison of the world's different political systems is centered on the similarities and differences between democracy and tyranny.

*Monarchy*

Different forms of democracy have been discussed, but there are also different forms of tyranny. Throughout history the most common form of tyrannical government was the monarchy. This system was usually based on inherited power, and it concentrated influence and authority in the hands of a small elite. Countries were ruled by a single person, often known as a king, emperor, or sultan. Monarchy still exists in the world today. Many European states and Japan continue to have ceremonial monarchs. These countries are democracies and the monarchies are not tyrannical. The ruler often serves as the head of state and presides over official functions but has very little real political power or influence. In the past, monarchs claimed their political authority through the divine right of kings, but in the contemporary world, most people believe in the social contract and that authority comes from the people, as is the case in democratic systems.

Great Britain's system of constitutional monarchy is one of the best examples of this form of government. The monarch, currently Queen Elizabeth II, presides over ceremonies and various formal events. She also has a consultative role with the prime minister and is the official chief of the military. Nonetheless, the monarch has almost no influence on the day-to-day operations of the government or deliberations of parliament. In most democratic systems that are based on the presidential model, the president or chief executive is the head of state. In addition, some countries, such as Germany, have an elected president who is the head of state, but not the nation's chief executive. While the chief executive presides over the day-to-day operations of the government, the head of state's duties are mainly ceremonial. For instance, the president represents the government at official functions.

There are a small number of countries around the world that still are monarchies in the traditional sense in that the rulers continue to possess considerable political power. Many countries in the Middle East, including Saudi Arabia, Jordan, Oman, Kuwait, and Qatar, are still ruled by monarchs. In addition, the tiny states of Brunei and Tonga in the Pacific are still monarchies, as are the African states of Morocco and Swaziland.

## Dictatorship

Like monarchies, dictatorships involve rule by a single individual. Unlike monarchies, dictatorships are usually not inherited. In addition, dictators rarely rely on the divine right of kings. Instead, in an argument similar to those made in favor of democracy, a dictator often claims to be a representative of the people who rules for the common good. Unlike the leaders of democracies, dictators are not elected (even though they often stage fake elections in an effort to increase their legitimacy) or responsible to the people.

# The Divine Right
# of Kings

In a speech to Parliament on March 21, 1609, King James I of England described the main arguments for the divine right of kings. Most of these arguments run counter to modern ideas of democracy:

> The state of monarchy is the supremest thing upon earth . . . Kings are justly called Gods, for that they exercise a manner or resemblance of divine power upon earth. For if you will consider the attributes to God, you shall see how they agree in the person of a king. God has power to create, or destroy, make, or unmake at his pleasure, to give life, or send death, to judge all, and to be judged nor accountable to none: to raise low things, and to make high things low at his pleasure, and to God are both soul and body due. And the like power have Kings; they make and unmake their subjects: they have power of raising, and casting down: of life, and of death: judges over all their subjects, and in all causes, and yet accountable to none but God only.

Dictators concentrate power in their own hands and allow very little freedom or liberty to their people. While democratic governments rely on the support of the people, dictators usually have to use the military or police forces to remain in power. Their opponents are often jailed, tortured, killed, or forced into exile. In democratic countries, on the other hand, the opponents of a government can even serve in the same legislature that provides the basis for the government as long as those opponents participate in the political process in a legitimate manner.

*Theocracy*

*Theocracy* translates from Greek as "government of God." Theocracies are political systems in which the government endeavors to rule based on religious principles. Early examples of theocracies included ancient Israel, Egypt, and even Rome. In the contemporary world, several regimes in the Middle East govern as theocracies, with their country's legal and political systems based on Islamic law (known as Sharia). On the one hand, theocracy is not incompatible with democracy. Modern theocracies, such as Iran, do have democratic elections and a representative assembly. However, the power of the Iranian parliament is limited in that its laws and policies cannot conflict with Sharia. Hence, unlike the accepted practice in most modern full democracies, there is no separation between church and state. In addition, most full democracies embrace religious freedom for all citizens, but freedom of religion is curtailed in theocracies.

## TOTALITARIAN REGIMES

Dictatorships are often totalitarian regimes. A totalitarian regime is one in which the government controls all aspects of a citizen's life. Unlike democracies in which people enjoy a high degree of personal and group liberty, totalitarianism attempts to impose a specific political and social culture that forces a sameness upon its citizens. Even social interactions and family life are supervised by the government. Examples of totalitarian regimes in the twentieth century include Nazi Germany under Adolf Hitler, the Soviet Union under Josef Stalin, and Communist China under Mao Zedong.

Totalitarian states outlaw all or most independent organizations. Everything is controlled by the state, including businesses and employment, clubs, civic groups, churches, and even family life. Loyalty to the government is enforced through the use of spies, secret police,

# The Constitution of Iran

The constitution of Iran establishes the country as a theocracy based on Islamic law as stated in the Muslim holy book, the Qur'an. Article 2 contains the constitutional basis for the theocracy:

Article 2
The Islamic Republic is a system based on belief in:

1. The One God (as stated in the phrase "There is no god except Allah"), His exclusive sovereignty and the right to legislate, and the necessity of submission to His commands;

2. Divine revelation and its fundamental role in setting forth the laws;

3. The return to God in the Hereafter, and the constructive role of this belief in the course of man's ascent towards God;

4. The justice of God in creation and legislation;

5. Continuous leadership (imamah) and perpetual guidance, and its fundamental role in ensuring the uninterrupted process of the revolution of Islam;

6. The exalted dignity and value of man, and his freedom coupled with responsibility before God; in which equity, justice, political, economic, social, and cultural independence, and national solidarity are secured by recourse to:

1. Continuous ijtihad of the fuqaha' possessing necessary qualifications, exercised on the basis off [sic] the Qur'an and the Sunnah of the Ma'sumun, upon all of whom be peace;

2. Sciences and arts and the most advanced results of human experience, together with the effort to advance them further;

3. Negation of all forms of oppression, both the infliction of and the submission to it, and of dominance, both its imposition and its acceptance.

In communist states, power is centralized. Mao Zedong was the leader of the Chinese Communist revolution and the leader of the Republic of China for almost forty years.

and informants within society. People who are disloyal or who criticize the government are often severely punished, and the government typically maintains an extensive system of prisons.

One other key difference between totalitarian systems and democracies is the extraordinary degree of control that the government exercises over the economy. Instead of allowing the economy to operate according to market principles, the government endeavors to set specific economic goals. It usually dictates wages and often forces people into certain jobs if it is determined that the society needs workers in those fields. Such economic control has proven to be counterproductive. Totalitarian regimes were unable to compete economically with free market democracies. For instance, the Soviet Union was unable to keep pace with the United States during the Cold War (1945–1989). Eventually the Soviet system collapsed and was replaced by a democratic system in Russia and in many of the countries that emerged from the former Soviet empire.

*Communism*
The Soviet Union was a communist, totalitarian regime. Communism is a political system based on the concept that true equality in a society can occur only when there is no private ownership of property or businesses, including homes, farms, factories, or stores. Instead, all wealth is divided equally so that the result is a society with no class or wealth differences. Variations of communism have been around for most of history. Scholars and philosophers such as Plato, St. Thomas Aquinas (1225–1274), and Thomas More (1478–1535) all wrote about versions of communism as an ideal society. Communism is in direct contrast to the ideas of democratic thinkers such as John Locke and Adam Smith, and it runs counter to the principles of free market democracy.

Modern communism is based on the work of Karl Marx (1818–1883), who argued that communism marked the final stage of history and the triumph of workers and the poor over the wealthy and elites. Following the Russian Revolution (1917), the Russians brought together a number of countries into a unity government known as the Soviet Union. The Soviets clamped down on political opposition, abolished religious freedom, and outlawed private property as part of an effort to establish a totalitarian regime. The Soviet system developed into an almost exact opposite of American-style free market democracy.

# The Soviet Constitution

The Soviet Constitution of 1977 reaffirmed the dominance of communism in Russia and the Soviet republics. Articles 6 through 8 describe the central role of the Communist Party in society and the importance of various parts of society in supporting communist ideology:

Article 6

(1) The leading and guiding force of the Soviet society and the nucleus of its political system, of all state organizations and public organizations, is the Communist Party of the Soviet Union [CPSU]. The CPSU exists for the people and serves the people.
(2) The Communist Party, armed with Marxism-Leninism, determines the general perspectives of the development of society and the course of the home and foreign policy of the USSR, directs the great constructive work of the Soviet people, and imparts a planned, systematic and theoretically substantiated character to their struggle for the victory of communism.
(3) All party organizations shall function within the framework of the Constitution of the USSR.

Article 7

Trade unions, the All-Union Leninist Young Communist League cooperatives, and other public organizations, participate, in accordance with the aims laid down in their rules, in managing state and public affairs, and in deciding political, economic, and social an [sic] cultural matters.

Article 8

(1) Work collectives take part in discussing and deciding state and public affairs, in planning production and social development, in training and placing personnel, and in discussing and deciding matters pertaining to the management of enterprises and institutions, and the use of funds allocated both for developing production and for social and cultural purposes and financial incentives.

(2) Work collectives promote socialist emulation, the spread of progressive methods of work, and the strengthening of production discipline, educate their members in the spirit of communist morality, and strive to enhance their political consciousness and raise their cultural level and skills and qualifications.

There were no true elections in which candidates were freely chosen, and people had limited freedom and liberty and almost no property. Also, the government tried to plan and manage the economy down to the smallest detail. Countries within the Soviet Union, and those ruled by the Soviets in Central and Eastern Europe, began a transition period after 1989 in which most adopted democracy and free market capitalism. It is important to note that democracy itself is not incompatible with communism, but many of the main concepts that define modern democracies, including the right to private property, are not. In addition, no communist country has yet implemented democracy and maintained its communist principles; once voters have a choice they have thus far rejected communist systems.

*Socialism*
Socialism shares many of the same principles as communism although it is less intrusive and oppressive. Like communism, socialism rejects any absolute right to private property and, therefore, runs counter to one of the main principles of modern, full democracies. Socialism also holds that the government should be in charge of overseeing and managing the economy. In return for government control of the economy, the state provides basic needs for its citizens, including education, health care, and employment. Socialist systems can range from totalitarian regimes to democracies, although these restrictions on property rights prevent socialist systems from being full democracies.

A combination of democracy and socialism has emerged in Western Europe and is known as social democracy (or sometimes a mixed economy). These systems are representative democracies, but the governments take much greater roles in managing the economy than do the governments of countries such as the United States. Often, social democracy is marked mainly by government ownership of major industries and businesses alongside privately owned corporations within the country. Social democracies also tend to have a much greater extent of social services, including government-controlled health care. ...ue that only countries that provide such services to ...ruly be considered full democracies.

# 7

## Democracy, Today and Tomorrow ▮▮▬

DEMOCRACY IS THE MOST COMMON political system in the world today. However, a range of challenges and issues still confront the expansion of this form of government. Many countries have experienced persistent problems as they endeavor to move from nondemocratic to democratic systems. Even in full democracies there continue to be lingering difficulties in ensuring minority rights and expanding economic and political access to disadvantaged groups. In addition, the freedoms inherent in democracies have led many people to decry the erosion of societal values and morals as governments try to balance the rights of the individual and the common good. Finally, the threat of terrorism has led democratic governments to limit freedoms in order to protect societies.

### NEW DEMOCRACIES

Since the end of the cold war, many countries have moved from nondemocratic to democratic systems. The change has been most marked in Europe and Latin America. In both areas, countries ruled by dictatorships and totalitarian regimes have given way to limited and full democracies. The demise of the Soviet Union, and its military and economic support for communist regimes around the world, was one of the main reasons for the emergence of many new democracies. With the end of the Cold War, many historians, philosophers, socialists, and political scientists heralded the triumph of free market democracy and predicted a new age of global politics marked by the spread of democracy and freedom. However, a number of problems have emerged, even in those countries that have become full democracies.

*Transition Problems*

The post–1989 new democracies of the world faced many similar problems. First, many states had little experience with democracy, and their political culture had to be reoriented. People had to learn how democracy works and to accept concepts such as minority rights. For instance, many people in the Baltic countries (Latvia, Lithuania, and Estonia) resented ethnic Russians because of the period of Soviet occupation. Second, their economic systems were often based on communism or socialism, and it was difficult to change to a free market economy. Often the establishment of market-driven economies resulted in the rise in the number of poor. In many countries in eastern and central Europe, unemployment became a real problem. After having an economic system in which everyone had a job, by 2004, unemployment in Poland reached a record 20 percent. Third, the elites who dominated the nondemocratic systems often retained political power during the democratic transition. This made it difficult for citizens to trust the new governments. For example, the president of Russia, Vladimir Putin, was a member of the Soviet secret police. Fourth, some countries, such as Russia, had to cope with a loss of international power and prestige. This undermined democratic institutions and made some people yearn for a return to the past in which their country was a world power.

*Promoting Democracy*

An important aspect of the spread of democracy after 1989 was the influence of powerful democracies around the world, led by the United States, and a range of international organizations. Both individual countries and international bodies such as the European Union (EU) and the United Nations (UN) devoted considerable resources to spreading democracy. These resources included billions of dollars in aid and technical assistance. There were also a number of incentives for countries to accept democracy.

The EU is a regional organization of twenty-five democratic member states in Europe. It removes trade barriers between countries

The fall of communism was not universally praised. Russia sank into an economic depression when the Soviet Union fell. Here, homeless Russians wait in line for a meal at an American-Russian charity.

and promotes political, economic, and social integration between the member countries. After the end of the Cold War, many countries that had been controlled by the Soviet Union keenly wanted to join the EU to gain the benefits of membership. However, in order to join, aspirant countries were required by the EU to adopt a range of reforms, including democratization and acceptance of EU standards on human rights and civil liberties. Countries also had to settle any border disputes with neighboring states. In 2004, the EU expanded from fifteen to twenty-five members; eight of the ten new members were newly democratic states, including the Czech Republic, Estonia, Hungary, Latvia, Lithuania, Poland, Slovakia, and Slovenia.

Central to these reforms is the adoption of the European Human Rights Convention. The convention contains a number of specific rights, including the right to life, to liberty and security, to marry, to receive a fair and just trial, and to privacy. The convention also has broad freedoms that were guaranteed, such as the freedom of expression, of association and assembly, and of religion. There are also specific prohibitions against torture, slavery and forced labor, discrimination,

# Countries That Changed to Full Democracies Since 1989

Bulgaria

Chile

Croatia

Czech Republic

Estonia

Hungary

Latvia

Lithuania

Moldova

Nicaragua

Paraguay

Philippines

Poland

Romania

Slovakia

Slovenia

and punishment without the due process of law. The convention outlaws the death penalty. In cases of violations of these rights, there is a special judicial body, the European Court of Human Rights, that hears cases. In this way, if a government is involved in violating a person's or group's rights, there is a court that is independent of, and has authority over, that government. When governments adopt the convention, they have to accept the authority of the Court. Currently, there are forty-one countries and 800 million people who officially adhere to the convention.

The UN was formed in 1945 to promote world peace, democracy, and prosperity. In 2006, it had 192 members. The organization is divided into numerous bureaus and agencies. One body, the World Food Program, provided $2.9 billion in food for ninety-six million people in more than eighty countries. The UN helps promote democracy by providing monitors to ensure free and fair elections in countries and through training and education. For instance, the UN oversaw the first free presidential elections in the history of Afghanistan in 2004.

One motivation for countries and organizations to promote democracy is that democratic countries tend to be less warlike than tyrannical or totalitarian regimes. For instance, after centuries of warfare in western Europe, countries such as France, Germany, Italy, and the United Kingdom now enjoy peaceful and close relations with one another. Proponents of democracy hope that conflict in other regions can also be lessened through the spread of democracy. This is especially true in regions such as Africa and the Middle East.

*The Growth of Antidemocratic Forces*
There has been a backlash against democratic movements in some nondemocratic areas. Opponents of democracy have complained that the system provides excessive personal freedom, which undermines local culture and morality. For instance, in some Islamic societies, such as Iran and Saudi Arabia, women have constraints on their civil rights. In certain countries women are still not allowed to vote, while in others they may not even be allowed to hold a job or appear in public without covering their faces. Opponents of democracy and Western culture have appealed to people's fears over the loss of Islamic identity and culture as a means to rally opposition to Western-style democracy. This is in spite of the fact that surveys and polls consistently demonstrate

# The European Convention on Human Rights (1950)

Similar in scope to the U.S. Bill of Rights, the European Convention on Human Rights covers civil liberties for most of the countries of Europe and all of the members of the European Union. The convention exists in addition to other national laws that provide civil rights and liberties. The following articles provide the main basis for civil liberties:

Article 9
1) Everyone has the right to freedom of thought, conscience and religion; this right includes freedom to change his religion or belief, and freedom, either alone or in community with others and in public or private, to manifest his religion or belief, in worship, teaching, practice and observance.
2) Freedom to manifest one's religion or beliefs shall be subject only to such limitations as are prescribed by law and are necessary in a democratic society in the interests of public safety, for the protection of public order, health or morals, or the protection of the rights and freedoms of others.

Article 10
1) Everyone has the right to freedom of expression. This right shall include freedom to hold opinions and to receive and impart information and ideas without interference by public authority and regardless of frontiers. This article shall not prevent States from requiring the licensing of broadcasting, television or cinema enterprises.
2) The exercise of these freedoms, since it carries with it duties and responsibilities, may be subject to such formalities, conditions, restrictions or penalties as are prescribed by law and are necessary in a democratic society, in the interests of national security,

territorial integrity or public safety, for the prevention of disorder or crime, for the protection of health or morals, for the protection of the reputation or the rights of others, for preventing the disclosure of information received in confidence, or for maintaining the authority and impartiality of the judiciary.

Article 11
1) Everyone has the right to freedom of peaceful assembly and to freedom of association with others, including the right to form and to join trade unions for the protection of his interests.
2) No restrictions shall be placed on the exercise of these rights other than such as are prescribed by law and are necessary in a democratic society in the interests of national security or public safety, for the prevention of disorder or crime, for the protection of health or morals or for the protection of the rights and freedoms of others. This article shall not prevent the imposition of lawful restrictions on the exercise of these rights by members of the armed forces, of the police or of the administration of the State.

Article 12
Men and women of marriageable age have the right to marry and to found a family, according to the national laws governing the exercise of this right.

that most Muslims prefer democracy. For instance, the World Values Study of 2002 found that 87 percent of Muslims thought democracy was the best form of government. However, radical extremists often portray the establishment of democracy as being synonymous with the decline of Islam and are able to garner support even from those who in principle support more freedom in government. One result is that democracy has consistently had difficulty taking root in Islamic countries.

## CONTINUING PROBLEMS FOR DEMOCRACIES

Even full democracies have continuing problems that could undermine the future of their political systems. One of the core principles of full democracy is the notion of equality. However, in almost all democracies, even modern, full democracies, there continue to be broad disparities in wealth and social status among different groups. Often those groups that face continuing discrimination and inequality are ethnic minorities and women. As a result, many democracies are experimenting with a variety of policies and programs designed to help disadvantaged groups.

*Affirmative Action*

Affirmative action is a range of policies designed to give preferences in fields such as education, employment, and political office to members of historically disadvantaged groups in a broad effort to promote equality. Affirmative action programs began in the United States as early as World War II (1939–1945), but it was not until the 1970s that the programs became widespread. In the United States, the primary focus of affirmative action programs have been racial and ethnic minorities, although some programs also exist specifically to help women. Affirmative action is not a quota system (in other words, these programs do not require that a certain percentage of employees or students be from a certain race, ethnicity, or gender). Instead, the policies often provide additional aid or assistance to job or school applicants. This aid may be in the form of specific preparation programs or may include additional points if employment or selection is based on a point system.

Many other countries have begun to implement American-style affirmative action programs as a way to uplift disadvantaged minority groups. In the 1990s, the EU began system-wide programs to help women. The EU also funds special training programs to aid women, ethnic groups, and minorities. There is even political affirmative action as in the aforementioned system whereby racial minorities may be granted a minimum number of seats in representative assemblies. Other countries, including Brazil, have begun to use American-style affirmative action as a way to increase minority student numbers in higher education. Ultimately, all of these programs have a similar interest in promoting the common good and protecting minority rights. Critics of affirmative action charge that the policies are a form of reverse discrimination that unfairly punish the majority. Partially in recognition of this notion, in 2004, the U.S. Supreme Court issued a decision that called for affirmative action to be phased out over a twenty-five-year period.

Thousands marched in Detroit in support of the University of Michigan's affirmative action programs. In June 2003, the Supreme Court voted to narrowly affirm the university's policy.

(Left to right) The Reverend Al Sharpton, recording artist Mary Blige, Martin Luther King III, and Hip-Hop mogul Russell Simmons, founder of Def Jam Records, join forces to launch "Rap the Vote 2000" in New York on May 31, 2000. The aim was to persuade urban youth to vote in large numbers.

*Voter Apathy*

A growing problem for many democracies is voter apathy, or citizen disinterest in politics. Democracy needs citizen participation in order to function. Citizens must give their representatives direction and clues about policy choices. They must also participate in efforts to launch referendums and recalls. Most importantly, citizens must vote in order for democracies to function. However, voter participation has been on the decline throughout the world. By the early 2000s, most full democracies had witnessed declines in voter turnout.

This decline is most pronounced in the United States. Since 1960, voter turnout has declined. By the 1990s, voter participation in national elections had fallen to less than 50 percent. In state and local elections, turnout has often been as low as 25 percent. This means that only a small number of Americans were making the major decisions about representation and policy choices for the rest of the nation (surveys show that older white males are the most likely to vote in the United States). Nor is the United States the only country to face such declines. For instance, in Europe during the 2004 EU parliament elections, voter turnout in many countries was less than 30 percent. In order to prevent voter apathy, some countries have compulsory voting, which means that all citizens are required by law to vote. Failure to vote usually results in fines. Countries such as Australia, Argentina, Belgium, Greece, and Singapore have compulsory voting. In Australia and Belgium, voter turnout averages 95 percent. Opponents of compulsory voting argue that such a system forces people to vote even though they may not know enough about the issues, and that such a system causes a backlash against the democratic system.

There are a variety of reasons for voter apathy. In some cases, people feel disconnected from the political process. They feel that elites control politics and that their vote does not count. In the United States, the electoral college often reinforces this notion. In addition, many citizens mistrust the government and believe there are high levels of corruption in politics. Finally, many people feel that there is little significant difference between major political parties in the United States and other full democracies. On the other hand, some scholars argue that voter apathy is the result of satisfaction. If people believe their lives are going well and their needs are met, they see little reason to participate in politics. In the 2004 U.S. presidential election, voter turnout increased to 59.4 percent, the highest level since 1968 (61.9 percent). Factors which increased turnout in the election include divided opinion over the war in Iraq and contention over domestic issues such as gay marriage (the presidential campaign also set records for spending on advertisements). This increase in voter turnout demonstrates that when campaigns attract people's attention and inspire them, they will vote.

## TERRORISM AND CIVIL LIBERTIES

Democratic countries such as the United States, Canada, Japan, and the European nations have strong commitments to civil rights enshrined in their constitutions. However, since the terrorist attacks on the United States on September 11, 2001, democratic governments have taken steps to limit some freedoms in order to maintain or increase security for their citizens. In many ways, this is a continuation of the debate between Locke and Rousseau over individual rights versus the common good: If someone is suspected of being a terrorist, even though there is no direct proof, it might be better for society if that person was arrested in order to prevent a future attack ("Better safe than sorry," as the expression goes). However, such arrests take away the individual freedom of all citizens by granting the government extraordinary powers. It may also be possible that innocent people would be arrested or put under suspicion.

Airport security in the United States is an example of this modern quandary. People have a constitutional right against unreasonable or unwarranted searches. On the other hand, the government has decided that the safety of airline passengers (and potentially other citizens who might suffer from a 9/11-style attack) outweighs that right of privacy and, therefore, anyone traveling on an airplane is subject to having his or her belongings and person searched. The courts have accepted the government's policy and argued that by purchasing an airline ticket, a person agrees to surrender his or her privacy rights. This continuing tension between public safety and personal freedom will remain a challenge for democracies.

## THE FUTURE OF DEMOCRACY

In spite of continuing challenges, many believe democracy is the freest and fairest system by which to organize governments. It is likely to continue to spread around the globe as more and more people begin to push for increased personal and cultural liberty. In addition, in most countries that have adopted democratic systems, the trend is toward increased democracy (moving from limited to full democracy, for instance) through greater civil liberties and civil rights.

Democracy has been embraced by most of the major world powers, countries such as the United States, Japan, India, and the European states. The most influential international organizations, including the UN and the EU, work to promote democratic governments. As time goes by, democratic states will continue to have to balance individual rights and civil liberties while they maintain the civil rights of minority groups and provide security and protection for their citizens. However, by allowing citizens to have the ultimate authority over policy, democracies seem to provide the best systems to debate, formulate, and implement policies that people will accept and embrace.

# Democracy and Other Governments

| DEMOCRACY | COMMUNISM | SOCIALISM |
|---|---|---|
| **Multiple legal political parties** | Only one legal political party (Communist Party) | Multiple legal political parties; limited electoral freedom |
| **Free rule by the people through elections** | No free elections; rule by a single individual or small group | Rule by people through elections, although individual or small group may dominate politics |
| **Opposition and dissent are accepted and may be encouraged** | Opposition and dissent are limited or forbidden | Opposition and dissent may be limited |
| **Private property protected by law and constitution** | No private property | Limited property rights |
| **Economy determined by free market** | State-controlled economy | Government has significant role in economy |
| **Unemployment determined mainly by the free market** | Officially no unemployment | Unemployment determined by combination of the free market and government policy |
| **Freedom of religion** | No freedom of religion | May have religious freedom |
| **Widespread and comprehensive civil liberties and civil rights; some social welfare** | Limited or no civil liberties or civil rights; widespread social welfare programs (such as free education and health care) | Civil liberties and civil rights may be curtailed by government, especially economic rights; widespread social welfare programs (such as free education, health care, and housing) |

| THEOCRACY | DICTATORSHIP | MONARCHY* |
| --- | --- | --- |
| Often only one legal political party | Often only one legal political party | May have no legal political parties, or only one |
| Limited or no electoral freedom; rule by a single individual or small group | Limited or no electoral freedom; rule by a single individual | Limited or no electoral freedom; rule by a single individual; monarchy may be hereditary or elective |
| Opposition and dissent are limited or forbidden | Opposition and dissent are limited or forbidden | Opposition and dissent may be limited or forbidden |
| Limited property rights | Limited property rights | Limited property rights, usually inherited; monarch may claim ownership of entire kingdom |
| Government may have a significant role in economy | Government may have significant role in economy | Government may have significant role in economy |
| Unemployment determined by free market and government policy | Unemployment determined by combination of the free market and government policy | Monarch may determine how people are to be employed; forced labor may be required |
| Religious worship limited to the state religion | Some religious freedom, if it does not threaten the regime | Religious freedom may be allowed if it does not threaten the regime—or not, depending on ruler |
| Limited or no civil liberties or civil rights; social welfare programs are limited | Limited or no civil liberties and civil rights; social welfare programs are limited | Social welfare programs may be limited |

*Monarchy here refers to absolute monarchy, the traditional form of monarchy known in many earlier kingdoms but rare today; modern constitutional monarchies are monarchies in name only and are typically governed as democratic or socialist republics.

# Timeline

**800–500 BCE**
Direct democracy is adopted as a form of government in Greek city-states such as Chios and Athens

**427–347 BCE**
Plato

**384–322 BCE**
Aristotle

**327 BCE**
Alexander the Great encounters limited, local democracies in India

**50 BCE–450 CE**
Limited, local democracies within the Roman Empire

**1200–1600**
Italian city-states, such as Florence, Genoa, and Venice, create limited democracies

**1215**
Magna Carta (Great Charter) signed in England

**1295**
Edward I of England calls the first Parliament

**1500–1650**
Protestant Reformation; leaders of the movement call for separation of church and state

**1607**
British colony founded at Jamestown in North America; colonists create a legislative assembly

**1620**
Colonists on their way to Massachusetts sign the Mayflower Compact, the first social contract in the North American colonies

**1632–1704**
John Locke

**1642–1651**
English Civil Wars result in the overthrow of the monarchy; when the monarchy is restored in 1660, it is a limited constitutional monarchy

**1689**
English Bill of Rights

**1689–1755**
Charles-Louis de Secondat, the Baron de Montesquieu

**1712–1788**
Jean-Jacques Rousseau

**1723–1790**
Adam Smith

**1743–1826**
Thomas Jefferson

**1751–1836**
James Madison

**1776**
Declaration of Independence (United States)

**1789**
Ratification of the U.S. Constitution and adoption of the Bill of Rights; Declaration of the Rights of Man (France)

**1799–1815**
Napoleonic era spreads French democratic ideals throughout Europe

**1848**
A series of democratic revolutions in Europe are defeated

**1870**
Fifteenth Amendment to the U.S. Constitution grants all male Americans the right to vote regardless of race or ethnicity; American states subsequently pass restrictive laws that limit the right to vote

**1893**
New Zealand becomes the first country to grant women the right to vote in the modern era

**1906**
Russia creates a representative assembly, the Duma

**1917**
Russian Revolution establishes the world's first national communist government

**1919**
Treaty of Versailles ends World War I and creates a number of new, democratic countries while replacing several monarchies with democracies; many of these countries, including Germany, become dictatorships in the 1920s and 1930s

**1920**
Women are granted the right to vote in the United States

**1945**
End of World War II; former fascist states of Japan, Germany, and Italy adopt democratic systems

**1947**
As the European empires decolonize, countries such as India become independent democracies; U.S. Marshall Plan offers economic incentives for European countries to adopt democracy

**1950s–1960s**
U.S. civil rights era leads to increased political rights for minorities

**1957**
The European Community (now the European Union) is created

**1989**
End of the Cold War; democracy spreads to former communist countries around the world

**1991**
First free and open presidential elections in Russian history; there are more democratic than nondemocratic countries in the world

**2000**
George W. Bush wins U.S. presidential election even though he loses the popular vote, creating new questions about the electoral college

**2001**
Terrorist attacks in the United States lead the country and many other full democracies to enact security measures that curtail some civil liberties

**2004**
Eight former communist countries join the European Union as full democracies

**2005**
First free national elections in Iraqi history

**2006**
Elections in the Democratic Republic of the Congo mark an end to decades of civil war

# Notes

**Chapter 1**

p. 9, Todd Landman. *Protecting Human Rights: A Comparative Study.* Washington, DC: Georgetown University Press, 2005, p. 1.

p. 9, Keith Faulks, Ken Phillips, and Alex Thompson. *Get Set for Politics.* Edinburgh: Edinburgh University Press, 2003, p. 74.

p. 9, Alan Ebenstein. *Introduction to Political Thinkers.* New York: Harcourt College Publishers, 2002, p. 248.

p. 12, Reo M. Christenson, Alan Engel, Dan Jacobs, Mostafa Rejai, and Herbert Waltzer. *Ideologies and Modern Politics,* 2nd ed. New York: Dodd, Mead and Company, 1975, pp. 185–186.

p. 12, Joseph F. Zimmerman. *The New England Town Hall Meeting: Democracy in Action.* Westport, CT: Praeger, 1999, p. 185.

pp. 12, 14, Todd Donovan and Shaun Bowler. "Direct Democracy and Minority Rights: An Extension." *American Journal of Political Science.* Vol. 42, No. 3 (July 1998), p. 1020.

pp. 12, 14, James Q. Wilson and John DiIulio Jr. *State and Local Government,* 3rd ed. Boston: Houghton Mifflin, 2001, p. 8.

pp. 14, 16, John F. Bibby. *Politics, Parties and Elections in*

*America*. Fourth Edition. Belmont, CA: Wadsworth Publishing, 2000, pp. 249–250.

p. 19, Robert Pastor and Qingshan Tan. "The Meaning of China's Village Elections." *The China Quarterly*. No. 162 (June 2000), p. 490.

p. 19, Kevin O'Brien. "Villagers, Elections and Citizenship in Contemporary China." *Modern China*. Vol. 27, No. 4 (October 2001), p. 408.

## Chapter 2

p. 23, Alan Ebenstein. *Introduction to Political Thinkers*. New York: Harcourt College Publishers, 2002, p. 59.

pp. 26, 28, Jeffrey Goldsworthy. *The Sovereignty of Parliament: History and Philosophy*. Oxford: Clarendon Press, 1999, p. 4.

p. 28, William A. Mueller. *Church and State in Luther and Calvin*. Nashville: Broadman, 1954, p. 24.

p. 28, Dean Hammer. *The Puritan Tradition in Revolutionary, Federalist and Whig Political Theory*. New York: Lang, 1998, 35.

p. 119: Insert: p. 29, Jacek Jeddruch. *Constitutions, Elections and Legislatures of Poland, 1493–1993*. Summit, NJ: EJJ Books, 1997, online at http://info-poland.buffalo.edu/JJ.html.

p. 32, Thomas Pangle. *The Spirit of Modern Republicanism: The Moral Vision of the American Founders and the Philosophy of Locke*. Chicago: University of Chicago Press, 1988, p. 30.

p. 32, Ruth Grant. *John Locke's Liberalism*. Chicago: University of Chicago Press, 1987, p. 9.

p. 35, Lois Schwoerer. "Locke, Lockean Ideas, and the Glorious Revolution." *Journal of the History of Ideas*. Vol. 51, No. 4 (October 1990), p. 532.

p. 35, Jonathan Marks. *Perfection and Disharmony in the Thought of Jean-Jacques Rousseau*. New York: Cambridge University Press, 2005, pp. 54–55.

p. 40, L. Nooman. *France: The Politics of Continuity and Change*. New York: Holt, Rinehart and Winston, 1970, p. 98.

p. 41, Christenson, Engel, Jacobs, Rejai, and Waltzer. *Ideologies and Modern Politics*, 2nd ed. New York: Dodd, Mead and Company, 1975, pp. 77–79.

## Chapter 3

pp. 43–44, Donald Gross. "Bicameralism and the Theory of Voting," *Western Political Quarterly*. Vol. 35, No. 4. (December 1982), p. 512.

pp. 46–47, Klaus von Beyne. *Parliamentary Democracy: Democratization, Destabilization, Reconsolidation, 1789–1999*. New York: St. Martin's Press, 2000, p. 207.

pp. 45, 48, John Kincaid. "Values and Tradeoffs in Federalism," *Publius*. Vol. 25, No. 2 (Spring 1995), pp. 31–32.

pp. 45, 48, Preston King. *Federalism and Federation*. Baltimore: Johns Hopkins University Press, 1983, p. 21.

pp. 50–51, Andrew C. McLaughlin. *The Confederation and the Constitution, 1783–1789*. New York: New York University Press, 1962, pp. 24–26.

p. 52, Keith Faulks, Ken Phillips, and Alex Thompson. *Get Set for Politics*. Edinburgh: Edinburgh University Press, 2003, pp. 90–91.

p. 54, James Q. Wilson and John DiIulio Jr. *State and Local Government*, 3rd ed. Boston: Houghton Mifflin, 2001, pp. 5–6.

pp. 54, 56, Aaron Wildavsky. "The Two Presidencies." In Steven Shull (ed.). *The Two Presidencies: A Quarter*

*Century Assessment.* Chicago: Nelson-Hall, 1991, pp. 11–25.

**Chapter 4**

pp. 58–59, Alan Ebenstein. *Introduction to Political Thinkers.* New York: Harcourt College Publishers, 2002, pp. 190–191.

p. 59, C.W. Cassinelli, "The 'Consent' of the Governed." *Western Political Quarterly.* Vol. 12, No. 2 (June 1959), pp. 391–392.

p. 59, Gus diZerega, "Liberalism, Democracy, and the State: Reclaiming the Unity of Liberal Politics." *The Review of Politics*, Vol. 63, No. 4 (Autumn 2001), p. 756.

p. 60, Ebenstein, p. 217.

pp. 59, 62, V. O. Key. *Public Opinion and American Democracy.* New York: Alfred Knopf, 1961, p. 20.

pp. 62–63, Kenneth Prewitt and Alan Stone. *The Ruling Elites: Elite Theory, Power, and American Democracy.* New York: Harper and Rowe, 1973, pp. 236–237.

p. 63, Lawrence J. R. Henson and John M. Bolland. *The Urban Web: Politics, Policy, and Theory*, 2nd ed. Chicago: Nelson-Hall, 1999, pp. 144–145.

pp. 64-65, U.S., Federal Elections Commission, "2004 Presidential Campaign Financial Activity Summarized." Washington, DC: GPO, 2005, online at http://www.fec.gov/press/press2005/20050203pressum/20050203pressum.html

p. 66, Robert L. Heilbroner. *The Worldly Philosophers: The Lives, Times and Ideas of the Great Economic Thinkers*, 6th ed. New York: Simon and Schuster, 1986, p. 55.

pp. 68–69, Kristjan Kristjansson. *Social Freedom: The Responsibility View.* New York: Cambridge University Press, 1996, pp. 48–50.

p. 71, Hans Blokland. *Freedom and Culture in Western Society*. New York: Routledge, 1997, pp. 184–185.

## Chapter 5

p. 73, James Q. Wilson and John Dilulio Jr. *State and Local Government*, 3rd ed. Boston: Houghton Mifflin, 2001, p. 26.

p. 76, Keith Faulks, Ken Phillips, and Alex Thompson. *Get Set for Politics*. Edinburgh: Edinburgh University Press, 2003, p. 75.

p. 76, Lawrence J. R. Henson and John M. Bolland. *The Urban Web: Politics, Policy, and Theory*, 2nd ed. Chicago: Nelson-Hall, 1999, p. 74.

pp. 76–77, Robert W. Jackson, "Political Elites, Mass Publics, and Support for Democratic Principles." *The Journal of Politics*, Vol. 34, No. 3 (August 1972), p. 756.

p. 80, Lanny W. Martin, "The Government Agenda in Parliamentary Democracies." *American Journal of Political Science*, Vol. 48, No. 3 (July 2004), p. 445.

pp. 81, 85, John F. Bibby. *Politics, Parties and Elections in America*. Fourth Edition. Belmont, CA: Wadsworth Publishing, 2000, pp. 276–278.

## Chapter 6

p. 88, Vernon Bogdanor. *The Monarchy and the Constitution*. Oxford: Clarendon Press, 1995, p. viii.

p. 89, King James I, "A Speech to the Lords and Commons of Parliament." London: March 21, 1609, online at http://www.luminarium.org/sevenlit/james/1609speech.htm

p. 90, Christenson, Engel, Jacobs, Rejai, and Waltzer. *Ideologies and Modern Politics*, 2nd ed. New York: Dodd, Mead and Company, 1975, pp. 52–53.

p. 90, Robert L. Heilbroner. *The Worldly Philosophers:*

*The Lives, Times and Ideas of the Great Economic Thinkers*, 6th ed. New York: Simon and Schuster, 1986, pp. 144–145.

p. 93, Shireen T. Hunter and Huma Malik, eds,. *Modernization, Democracy and Islam*. Westport, CT: Praeger, 2005, p. 15.

pp. 93, 96, Christenson, Engel, Jacobs, Rejai, and Waltzer, pp. 106–110.

p. 96, Keith Faulks, Ken Phillips, and Alex Thompson. *Get Set for Politics*. Edinburgh: Edinburgh University Press, 2003, p. 77.

p. 96, Larry Diamond. *Developing Democracy: Towards Consolidation*. Baltimore: Johns Hopkins University Press, 1999, p. 25.

## Chapter 7

p. 97, Richard Kerry. *The Star-Spangled Mirror: America's Image of Itself and the World*. Savage, MD: Rowman & Littlefield, 1990, p. 3.

p. 98, Stephen Haggard and Robert R. Kaufman. *The Political Economy of Democratic Transitions*. Princeton: Princeton University Press, 1995, p. 89.

pp. 98–99, Freedom House. *Freedom in the World*. May 2004. http://www.freedomhouse.org/

p. 108, Donald M. Snow. *United States Foreign Policy: Politics Beyond the Water's Edge*, 3rd ed. Belmont, CA: Wadsworth Publishing, 2005, p. 262.

p. 109, Anne M. Khadermian, "Homeland (In) Security." *In* Robert Maranto, Douglas M. Brattebo, and Tom Lansford, eds. *The Second Term of George W. Bush: Prospects and Perils*. New York: Palgrave Macmillan, 2006, p. 179.

# Further Information

**BOOKS**

Bachrach, Peter. *The Theory of Democratic Elitism*. Boston: Little, Brown and Company, 1967.

Bellamy, Richard, and Alex Warleigh, eds. *Citizenship and Governance in the European Union*. New York: Continuum, 2001.

Bryan, Frank M. *Real Democracy: The New England Town Hall Meeting and How it Works*. Chicago: University of Chicago Press, 2004.

Cashman, Sean Dennis. *African-Americans and the Quest for Civil Rights, 1900–1990*. New York: New York University Press, 1991.

Dahl, Robert A. *Democracy and Its Critics*. New Haven: Yale University Press, 1989.

Dione, E. J. *Why Americans Hate Politics*. New York: Simon and Schuster, 1992.

Genovese, Michael A., and Matthew J. Streb, eds. *Polls and Politics: The Dilemmas of Democracy*. Albany: State University of New York Press, 2004.

Jones, Nicholas F. *Rural Athens Under the Democracy*. Philadelphia: University of Pennsylvania Press, 2004.

Kaplan, Temma. *Taking Back the Streets: Women, Youth and Direct Democracy*. Berkeley: University of California Press, 2004.

Manhein, Jarol. *All of the People, All of the Time*. Armonk, NY: M. E. Sharpe, 1991.

Miroff, Bruce, Raymond Seidelman, and Todd Swanstrom, eds. *Debating Democracy: A Reader in American Politics*. Boston: Houghton Mifflin Company, 1997.

Montero, Alfred P., and David J. Samuels, eds. *Decentralization and Democracy in Latin America*. Notre Dame, IN: University of Notre Dame Press, 2004.

Rossilli, Mariagrazia, ed., *Gender Policies in the European Union*. New York: Peter Lang, 2000.

Sharma, J. P. *Republics in Ancient India, 1500 B.C.–500 B.C.* Leiden, The Netherlands: E. J. Brill, 1968.

Sheldon, Garret Ward, ed., *The Encyclopedia of Political Thought*. New York: Facts On File, 2001.

Weiss, Robert. *"We Want Jobs": A History of Affirmative Action*. New York: Garland, 1997.

Wood, Alan. *Asian Democracy in World History*. New York: Routledge, 2004.

## WEB SITES

**Center for the Evolution of Democracy**: this group endeavors to promote a greater understanding of demo-cracy and the challenges facing contemporary democratic systems
http://www.cedemocracy.org/engbrochure.html

**ElectionGuide.Org**: provides comprehensive information about elections all over the world, including results by country and past elections
http://www.electionguide.org

**Fair Vote: The Center for Voting and Democracy**: an organization that promotes equity in voting practices
http://www.fairvote.org/

**Freedom House**: Freedom House ranks countries according to their level of individual and governmental freedom in annual reports. It also details the political and civil rights of all of the countries of the world and issues special reports on contemporary issues
http://www.freedomhouse.org/

**International Institute for Democracy and Electoral Assistance (IDEA)**: an international body that seeks to aid countries in their transition to democracy, IDEA's Web site contains a range of information on democratic institutions
http://www.idea.int/about

**International Women's Democracy Center**: this organization provides detailed information about women and democracy, as well as the struggle for gender rights in the world
http://www.iwdc.org

**United States Department of State**: the U.S. State Department provides detailed information on the politics, economic systems, and human rights of individual countries
http://www.state.gov/r/pa/ei/bgn

**World Movement for Democracy**: examines the efforts to promote full democracy around the world
http://www.wmd.org

All Internet sites were accurate and available when sent to press.

# Bibliography

Barber, B. *Strong Democracy: Participatory Politics for a New Age*. Berkeley: University of California Press, 1984.

Bibby, John F. *Politics, Parties and Elections in America*. Fourth Edition. Belmont, CA: Wadsworth Publishing, 2000.

Blokland, Hans. *Freedom and Culture in Western Society*. New York: Routledge, 1997.

Cassinelli, C. W. "The 'Consent' of the Governed." *Western Political Quarterly*. Vol. 12, No. 2 (June 1959).

Bogdanor, Vernon. *The Monarchy and the Constitution*. Oxford: Clarendon Press, 1995.

Christenson, Reo M., Alan Engel, Dan Jacobs, Mostafa Rejai, and Herbert Waltzer. *Ideologies and Modern Politics*, 2nd ed. New York: Dodd, Mead and Company, 1975.

Cook, Brian. *Bureaucracy and Self-Government: Reconsidering the Role of Public Administration in American Politics*. Baltimore, MD: Johns Hopkins University, 1996.

Dahl, Robert. *Who Governs.* New Haven, CT: Yale University Press, 1961.

De Tocqueville, Alexis. *Democracy in America.* New York: Mentor Books, 1956.

Diamond, Larry. *Developing Democracy: Towards Consolidation.* Baltimore, MD: Johns Hopkins University Press, 1999.

DiZerega, Gus. "Liberalism, Democracy, and the State: Reclaiming the Unity of Liberal Politics." *The Review of Politics.* Vol. 63, No. 4 (Autumn 2001).

Donovan, Todd, and Shaun Bowler. "Direct Democracy and Minority Rights: An Extension." *American Journal of Political Science*, Vol. 42, No. 3 (July 1998).

Downs, Anthony. *An Economic Theory of Democracy.* New York: Harper & Row, 1957.

Dye, Thomas R. *American Federalism: Competition Among Governments.* Lexington, MA: Lexington Books, 1990.

Ebenstein, Alan. *Introduction to Political Thinkers.* New York: Harcourt College Publishers, 2002.

Eidelberg, Paul. *The Philosophy of the American Constitution.* New York: Free Press, 1968.

Farrar, Cynthia. *The Origins of Democratic Thinking.* Cambridge, UK: Cambridge University Press, 1988.

Faulks, Keith, Ken Phillips, and Alex Thompson. *Get Set for Politics*. Edinburgh: Edinburgh University Press, 2003.

Femia, Joseph V. *Marxism and Democracy*. Oxford: Clarendon Press, 1993.

Forsythe, David P., ed. *Human Rights in the New Europe: Problems and Progress*. Lincoln: University of Nebraska Press, 1994.

Freedom House. *Freedom in the World*. May 2004. http://www.freedomhouse.org/

Goldsworthy, Jeffrey. *The Sovereignty of Parliament: History and Philosophy*. Oxford: Clarendon Press, 1999.

Grant, Ruth. *John Locke's Liberalism*. Chicago: University of Chicago Press, 1987.

Gross, Donald. "Bicameralism and the Theory of Voting," *Western Political Quarterly*. Vol. 35, No. 4 (December 1982).

Haggard, Stephen, and Robert R. Kaufman. *The Political Economy of Democratic Transitions*. Princeton, NJ: Princeton University Press, 1995.

Hammer, Dean. *The Puritan Tradition in Revolutionary, Federalist and Whig Political Theory*. New York: Lang, 1998.

Hanes, Walton Jr., and Robert C. Smith. *American Politics and the African American Quest for Universal Freedom*. New York: Longman, 2000.

Heilbroner, Robert L. *The Worldly Philosophers: The Lives, Times and Ideas of the Great Economic Thinkers*, 6th ed. New York: Simon and Schuster, 1986.

Henson, Lawrence J. R., and John M. Bolland. *The Urban Web: Politics, Policy, and Theory*, 2nd ed. Chicago: Nelson-Hall, 1999.

Hunter, Shireen T., and Huma Malik, eds. *Modernization, Democracy and Islam*. Westport, CT: Praeger, 2005.

Jackson, Robert W. "Political Elites, Mass Publics, and Support for Democratic Principles." *The Journal of Politics.* Vol. 34, No. 3 (August 1972).

Kerry, Richard. *The Star-Spangled Mirror: America's Image of Itself and the World*. Savage, MD: Rowman & Littlefield, 1990.

Key, V. O. *Public Opinion and American Democracy*. New York: Alfred Knopf, 1961.

Khadermian, Anne M. "Homeland (In) Security." *In* Robert Maranto, Douglas M. Brattebo, and Kincaid, John. "Values and Tradeoffs in Federalism." *Publius*. Vol. 25, No. 2 (Spring 1995).

King, Preston. *Federalism and Federation*. Baltimore, MD: John Hopkins University Press, 1983.

Kristjansson, Kristjan. *Social Freedom: The Responsibility View*. New York: Cambridge University Press, 1996.

Landman, Todd. *Protecting Human Rights: A Comparative Study*. Washington, DC: Georgetown University Press, 2005.

Lansford, Tom, ed. *The Second Term of George W. Bush: Prospects and Perils*. New York: Palgrave Macmillan, 2006.

Larsen, J. A. O. *Representative Government in Greek and Roman History*. Berkeley: University of California Press, 1966.

Laswell, Harold. *Politics: Who Gets What, When and How*. New York: McGraw-Hill, 1938.

Marks, Jonathan. *Perfection and Disharmony in the Thought of Jean-Jacques Rousseau*. New York: Cambridge University Press, 2005.

Martin, Lanny W. "The Government Agenda in Parliamentary Democracies." *American Journal of Political Science*. Vol. 48, No. 3 (July 2004).

McLaughlin, Andrew C. *The Confederation and the Constitution, 1783–1789*. New York: New York University Press, 1962.

Mueller, William A. *Church and State in Luther and Calvin*. Nashville: Broadman, 1954.

Nooman, L. *France: The Politics of Continuity and Change*. New York: Holt, Rinehart and Winston, 1970.

O'Brien, Kevin. "Villagers, Elections and Citizenship in Contemporary China." *Modern China*. Vol. 27, No. 4 (October 2001).

Pangle, Thomas. *The Spirit of Modern Republicanism: The Moral Vision of the American Founders and the Philosophy of Locke*. Chicago: University of Chicago Press, 1988.

Parenti, Michael. *Democracy for the Few*, 7th ed. New York: St. Martin's Press, 2002.

Pastor, Robert, and Qingshan Tan. "The Meaning of China's Village Elections." *The China Quarterly*. No. 162 (June 2000).

Prewitt, Kenneth, and Alan Stone. *The Ruling Elites: Elite Theory, Power, and American Democracy*. New York: Harper and Row, 1973.

Sartori, Giovanni. *The Theory of Government Revisited*. Chatham, NJ: Chatham House, 1987.

Schwoerer, Lois. "Locke, Lockean Ideas, and the Glorious Revolution." *Journal of the History of Ideas*. Vol. 51, No. 4 (October 1990).

Snow, Donald M. *United States Foreign Policy: Politics Beyond the Water's Edge*, 3rd ed. Belmont, CA: Wadsworth Publishing, 2005.

Thurber, James. *Divided Democracy*. Washington, DC: CQ Press, 1991.

Tilly, Charles. *Contention and Democracy in Europe: 1650–2000*. New York: Cambridge University Press, 2004.

von Beyne, Klaus. *Parliamentary Democracy: Democratization, Destabilization, Reconsolidation, 1789–1999*. New York: St. Martin's Press, 2000.

West, Darrell, and Burdett Loomis. *The Sound of Money: How Political Interests Get What They Want*. New York: W. W. Norton, 1999.

Wildavsky, Aaron. "The Two Presidencies." In Steven Shull, ed. *The Two Presidencies: A Quarter Century Assessment*. Chicago: Nelson-Hall, 1991.

Wilson, James Q., and John Dilulio Jr. *State and Local Government*, 3rd ed. Boston: Houghton Mifflin, 2001.

Wood, Gordon. *The Creation of the American Republic*. Chapel Hill: University of North Carolina Press, 1969.

Wright, Deil. *Understanding Intergovernmental Relations*. Belmont, CA: Brooks/Cole, 1988.

Zakaria, Fareed. *The Future of Freedom: Illiberal Democracy at Home and Abroad*. New York: W. W. Norton, 2004.

Zimmerman, Joseph F. *The New England Town Hall Meeting: Democracy in Action*. Westport, CT: Praeger, 1999.

# INDEX

Page numbers in **boldface** are illustrations, tables, and charts.

# About the Author

Tom Lansford is the assistant dean of the College of Arts and Letters and an associate professor of political science at the University of Southern Mississippi. He is the author or editor of more than twenty books on politics, government, and international relations. *Communism* and *Democracy* in the Political Systems of the World series are his first books for Marshall Cavendish Benchmark. Dr. Lansford is also the author of more than one hundred encyclopedic entries, book chapters, and short essays. He lives in Long Beach, Mississippi.